总主编 文 旭

NEW WORLD
INTERACTIVE ENGLISH

新世界
交互英语 读写译 3 学生用书

主　编：刘　瑾
副主编：李江骅　罗红玲
编　者：（按姓氏笔画顺序）
　　　　于昌利　王　瑶　任尉香
　　　　刘　佳　何宇洪　张　颖

原版作者：Milada Broukal

清華大学出版社
北　京

Copyright © 2017 by National Geographic Learning, a Cengage company.
Original edition published by Cengage Learning. All Rights reserved.
本书原版由圣智学习出版公司出版。版权所有，盗印必究。

Tsinghua University Press is authorized by Cengage Learning to publish and distribute exclusively this adaptation edition. This edition is authorized for sale in the People's Republic of China only (excluding Hong Kong SAR, Macao SAR and Taiwan). Unauthorized export of this edition is a violation of the Copyright Act. No part of this publication may be reproduced or distributed by any means, or stored in a database or retrieval system, without the prior written permission of the publisher.
本改编版由圣智学习出版公司授权清华大学出版社独家出版发行。此版本仅限在中华人民共和国境内（不包括中国香港、澳门特别行政区及中国台湾）销售。未经授权的本书出口将被视为违反版权法的行为。未经出版者预先书面许可，不得以任何方式复制或发行本书的任何部分。

"National Geographic", "National Geographic Society" and the Yellow Border Design are registered trademarks of the National Geographic Society® Marcas Registradas.

Cengage Learning Asia Pte. Ltd.
151 Lorong Chuan, #02-08 New Tech Park, Singapore 556741
本书封面贴有 Cengage Learning 防伪标签，无标签者不得销售。

北京市版权局著作权合同登记号　图字：01-2016-8560

版权所有，侵权必究。举报：010-62782989，**beiqinquan@tup.tsinghua.edu.cn**。

图书在版编目（CIP）数据

新世界交互英语. 读写译学生用书. 3 / 文旭总主编；刘瑾主编. —北京：清华大学出版社，2017（2022.7重印）
ISBN 978-7-302-46294-1

Ⅰ.①新… Ⅱ.①文… ②刘… Ⅲ.①英语—阅读教学—高等学校—教材　②英语—写作—高等学校—教材　③英语—翻译—高等学校—教材　Ⅳ.①H319.39

中国版本图书馆 CIP 数据核字（2017）第 021457 号

责任编辑：蔡心奕
封面设计：子　一
责任校对：王凤芝
责任印制：丛怀宇

出版发行：清华大学出版社
　　　　网　　址：http://www.tup.com.cn, http://www.wqbook.com
　　　　地　　址：北京清华大学学研大厦 A 座　　邮　编：100084
　　　　社 总 机：010-83470000　　邮　购：010-62786544
　　　　投稿与读者服务：010-62776969, c-service@tup.tsinghua.edu.cn
　　　　质 量 反 馈：010-62772015, zhiliang@tup.tsinghua.edu.cn
印 装 者：山东临沂新华印刷物流集团有限责任公司
经　　销：全国新华书店
开　　本：210mm×285mm　　印　张：14.5　　字　数：408 千字
版　　次：2017 年 3 月第 1 版　　印　次：2022 年 7 月第 8 次印刷
定　　价：56.00 元

产品编号：071685-02

PREFACE

《国家中长期教育改革和发展规划纲要（2010—2020年）》明确指出，要"适应国家经济社会对外开放的要求，培养大批具有国际视野、通晓国际规则、能够参与国际事务和国际竞争的国际化人才"。《大学英语教学指南》提出，"大学英语课程应根据本科专业类教学质量国家标准，参照本指南进行合理定位，服务于学校的办学目标、院系人才培养的目标和学生个性化发展的需求"。

《新世界交互英语》是清华大学出版社站在国家外语教育与人才培养的战略高度，从美国圣智学习出版公司引进优质原版素材、精心打造出版的一套通用大学英语教材。为满足国内大学英语教学的实际需要，出版社邀请国内多所大学，在《大学英语教学指南》的指导下，对原版教材进行了改编。本套教材汇集全球顶尖品牌教学资源，贯彻启发性教学理念，以课堂教学为纽带，将全球化视野与学生真实生活联系起来，注重学生个性化发展需求，力求培养具有较高英语应用能力和跨文化交际能力的国际化人才。

一、教材特色

本套教材主要有以下特色：

❶ 素材来源：汇集全球顶尖品牌教学资源

本套教材的素材源自全球两大顶尖品牌教学资源：美国国家地理（National Geographic Learning）和TED演讲（TED Talks），为学生提供了大量原汁原味的视频、音频和图片，将世界各地的自然风光、风土人情、文化习俗带进课堂，以拓展学生的思维，并拓宽他们的国际化视野，从而达到提高学生语言应用能力和跨文化交际能力之目的。

❷ 编写理念：倡导启发性教学

本套教材将全球真实事件和精彩观点引入教学，结合中国传统文化和国情，注重思维训练，启发思考，以帮助学生理解中西文化差异，在培养学生听说读写译等英语应用能力的同时，着力培养其国际视野和创新精神，实现学生的全面发展。

❸ 核心目标：用课堂连接世界与学生生活

本套教材以课堂教学为纽带，将多姿多彩的世界万象与触手可及的学生生活连接起来，让学生具有全球化视野的同时，关注自身生活，思考中国问题，并学会用英语去表达自己的思想，从而成长为兼具扎实英语基本功和敏锐批判性思维的国际化人才。

二、改编思路

中方编写团队在对原版教材进行本土化改编过程中，做了适当的增补、替换和删减等工作。主要改编思路如下：

❶ 增补中国文化和中国国情内容

本教材注重培养学生对中国传统文化的认同，着力培养学生使用英语介绍中国文化的能力。在问题设计、练习改编方面重视本土问题，以帮助学生理解中西文化差异；在翻译、写作、口语活动中融入文化对比的元素，启迪学生对本土文化进行思考，培养其国际视野和中国情怀。

❷ 设计实用型和兴趣型练习

在设计练习时，适当参考了雅思、托福、大学英语四六级考试的题型，补充了更多的听力、翻译等练习，增强了教材的实用性；同时，结合时代发展，我们在"读写译"系列中加入扫描二维码以获取更多主题阅读材料的新元素，以充分调动学生的学习兴趣和求知欲望，使他们在主动学习的过程中提高英语水平和综合素养。

❸ 引入批判性思维训练和创新写作题型

本教材注重引导学生正确区分人物与观点、事实与解释、审美与判断、语言与现实、字面义与隐含义等，对问题进行批判性评价。"读写译"系列教材每个单元专门设计了一项针对批判性思维训练的练习，根据阅读模块内容启迪学生深度思考，进而提出独到见解；在写作能力培养上，设计了环环相扣、逻辑紧密的练习，体裁题材多样，积极鼓励创新写作，实现批判思维与创新写作的结合。

三、教材结构

本套教材分为"视听说"和"读写译"两个独立系列，每个系列包含学生用书和教师用书各四个级别。每个级别包含八个单元，每个单元可供四课时使用。

其中，"视听说"每个单元包含两大部分。第一部分主要围绕音频素材展开，包含A、B、C、D四个板块，分别对应四个教学目标（Goals）。第二部分的E、F两个板块主要包括视频素材和拓展练习，每个单元均包含美国国家地理录像视频Video Journal和拓展练习Further Practice，每两个单元之后含一个TED Talks视频。

"读写译"每个单元包含Reading、Writing和Translation三个部分。Reading部分包含两篇课文；Writing部分介绍若干个Writing Skills；Translation部分包含汉译英和英译汉两个篇章翻译练习。每个单元最后都设计了Weaving It Together综合和拓展板块，用以培养学生课下自学能力。

四、适用对象

本套教材适用于我国高校各层次公共英语和英语专业基础技能课程教学，同时也适用于成人自学。

五、编写团队

本套教材的总主编为西南大学文旭教授。"视听说"1-4册主编分别为莫启扬、孙阳、李成坚、段满福；"读写译"1-4册主编分别为崔校平、姜毓锋、刘瑾、马刚。来自全国近十所高校的几十名专家和骨干教师参与了本套教材的设计和编写，美国圣智学习出版公司的英语教育专家和教材编写专家对全书进行了审定。

在改编之前，我们广泛咨询了国内外英语教育领域的资深专家学者，开展了充分的调研和分析，确定了本套教材的改编理念和方案，最终使本套教材得以与广大师生见面。教材的改编凝聚了诸多专家学者的经验和智慧。在此，对为本套教材的改编和出版付出辛勤劳动的所有老师以及出版社的各位同仁表示衷心的感谢。由于水平有限，不足之处在所难免。我们真诚地希望大家提出宝贵意见，并在未来的修订中使之更趋完善。

文旭

2017年2月

UNIT WALK-THROUGH

Stunning **National Geographic images** introduce the unit theme and readings.

Theme-based units combine reading and writing through a balanced and engaging process designed to integrate the two effectively.

Pre-Reading activities prepare students by introducing key concepts and vocabulary from the readings.

Engaging readings motivate students to become better readers.

Post-Reading **vocabulary activities** recycle target vocabulary, building students' word knowledge.

Students look for the reading's main ideas and details to develop **key reading skills**.

Critical Thinking section challenges students to analyze, synthesize, and critically evaluate ideas and information in each reading.

Unit Walk-Through v

UNIT WALK-THROUGH

Writing Skills provide students with essential tools for composition.

Writing Practice section activates the writing skills taught and guides students through the writing process.

Translation section provides two C-E and E-C passages related to Chinese and Western culture, helping students develop their translation skills and intercultural competence.

Weaving It Together section includes Unit Project and Internet research activities, as well as extra theme-related readings, expanding students' knowledge of the unit theme and further developing their reading, writing, and research skills.

Unit Walk-Through   vii

CONTENTS

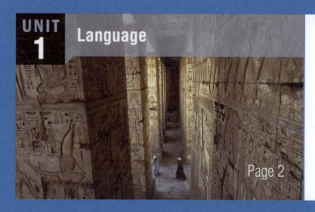

UNIT 1 — Language — Page 2

- **Reading 1**   Spell It in English
- **Reading 2**   "Jumbo"
- **Writing**   The Process Essay | Time Expressions
- **Translation**
- **Weaving It Together**

UNIT 2 — Hygiene — Page 28

- **Reading 1**   How Clean Is Clean?
- **Reading 2**   Bathing Japanese Style
- **Writing**   Pre-Writing Techniques | Definitions | The Definition Essay
- **Translation**
- **Weaving It Together**

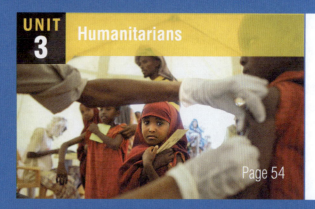

UNIT 3 — Humanitarians — Page 54

- **Reading 1**   John Bul Dau and the "Lost Boys of Sudan"
- **Reading 2**   Patrick Meier, Crisis Mapper
- **Writing**   Paraphrasing | Simile and Metaphor in a Description Essay
- **Translation**
- **Weaving It Together**

UNIT 4 — Psychology — Page 78

- **Reading 1**   What Our Bodies Say About Us
- **Reading 2**   Why We Are What We Are
- **Writing**   Writing a Summary | The Principle of Classification | The Classification Essay
- **Translation**
- **Weaving It Together**

UNIT 5 — Gender

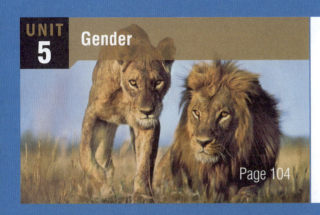

Page 104

- **Reading 1** Males and Females: What's the Difference?
- **Reading 2** Life Chances
- **Writing** How to Quote | Comparison and Contrast | The Comparison-and-Contrast Essay | Comparison-and-Contrast Indicators
- **Translation**
- **Weaving It Together**

UNIT 6 — Nutrition

Page 132

- **Reading 1** What's *Really* on Your Dinner Plate?
- **Reading 2** Hormones in Food: Should You Worry?
- **Writing** The Cause-and-Effect Essay
- **Translation**
- **Weaving It Together**

UNIT 7 — Issues for Debate

Page 158

- **Reading 1** Tweet Touches Off Heated Debate
- **Reading 2** Do Animals Have Rights?
- **Writing** The Argument Essay
- **Translation**
- **Weaving It Together**

UNIT 8 — Readings from Literature

Page 184

- **Reading 1** The Tell-Tale Heart
- **Reading 2** If
- **Writing** Narrator and Point of View | Writing an Analysis of a Short Story | Determining the Theme of a Poem
- **Translation**
- **Weaving It Together**

UNIT 1
Language

Hieroglyphics are sculpted into the walls of the Mortuary Temple of Ramesses III in Luxor, Egypt.

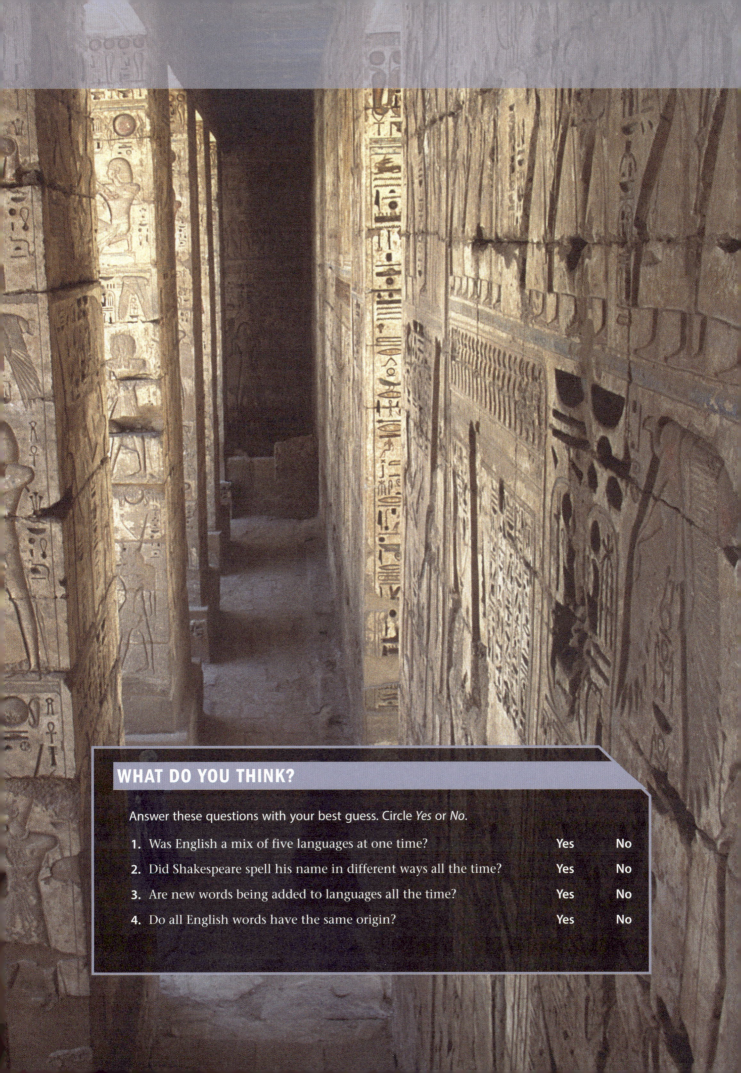

WHAT DO YOU THINK?

Answer these questions with your best guess. Circle *Yes* or *No*.

1. Was English a mix of five languages at one time?   Yes   No
2. Did Shakespeare spell his name in different ways all the time?   Yes   No
3. Are new words being added to languages all the time?   Yes   No
4. Do all English words have the same origin?   Yes   No

Reading 1

Pre-Reading

Preparing for the Reading Topic

A Discuss these questions with your classmates.

1. Do you think spelling rules are important? Why or why not?
2. What spelling rules do you know in English?
3. There were no spelling rules when Old English was spoken. What problems do you think this situation caused for people?

B Six words in the list below are spelled wrong. Find the misspelled words and correct them. Use a dictionary to check your answers.

1. pronunciation (the way you say a word) _____
2. batchelor (unmarried male) _____
3. superintendant (manager) _____
4. exerpt (selected passage from a book or film) _____
5. absorption (process of being absorbed) _____
6. tarrif (import fee) _____
7. occurence (happening) _____
8. newstand (place where you buy newspapers and magazines) _____
9. separate (to move apart) _____
10. nighttime (at night) _____

Key Vocabulary

As you read "Spell It in English", pay attention to the following words and phrases and see if you can work out their meanings from the contexts.

merging	gain momentum
evolved	philanthropist
indifferent	got carried away
liberal	onset
fanaticism	shed

A manuscript page of a poem, *The Siege of Thebes* by John Lydgate, written in fifteenth-century English

Spell It in English

1   English spelling is confusing and chaotic, as any student of English knows all too well. "How can the letters *ough* spell so many different sounding words," they ask, "like *dough*, *bough*, *rough*, and *through*?" And what about a word like *colonel*, which clearly contains no *r* yet pretends it does, and *ache*, with its *k* sound instead of the *chuh* sound of *arch*? And why does *four* have a *u* while *forty* doesn't? There are no simple rules for English spelling, but there is an explanation behind its complexity. We have only to look back in history.

2   Over the centuries, the English language has been like a magnet, attracting words from numerous other languages. It all started with the Britons, an ancient people living in a part of Western Europe that eventually became the British Isles[1]. The Britons spoke a language called Celtic[2], which was a combination of the early forms of Irish[3], Scottish[4], and Welsh[5]. When the Britons were conquered by the Romans and later the Germanic tribes, their language was also invaded. The **merging** of the languages gave birth to Old English (an early form of the Modern English we know), and a Latin[6] alphabet replaced, with a few exceptions, the ancient Germanic alphabet. In the ninth century, the conquering Norsemen from Scandinavia[7] added their pinch of language spice, as did the French in the 11th century.

---

1 the British Isles 不列颠群岛，包括大不列颠（英格兰、苏格兰、威尔士）、爱尔兰以及附近的小岛
2 Celtic 凯尔特语，印欧语系分支，包括爱尔兰语、苏格兰盖尔语、威尔士语、布列塔尼语、马恩岛语、康沃尔语以及几种已灭绝的前罗马时期语言，如高卢语
3 Irish 爱尔兰语
4 Scottish 苏格兰语
5 Welsh 威尔士语
6 Latin 拉丁语，古罗马的语言
7 Scandinavia 斯堪的纳维亚，由挪威、瑞典、丹麦，有时也包括冰岛、芬兰和法罗群岛组成的文化区

3   By the 14th century, English, with its mix of at least five languages, had **evolved** into what is called Middle English and had become Britain's official language. At that time, however, its spellings were far from consistent or rational. Many dialects had developed over the centuries, and sometimes people adopted the spelling used in one part of the country and the pronunciation used in another. For instance, today we use the western English spellings for *busy* and *bury*, but we give the first the London pronunciation *bizzy* and the second the Kentish[8] pronunciation *berry*. Of course, this all happened when English was primarily a spoken language, and only scholars knew how to read and write. Even they appear to have been quite **indifferent** to matters of consistency in spelling and were known to spell the same word several different ways in a single sentence.

4   Even after William Caxton[9] set up England's first printing press[10] in the late 15th century and the written word became available to everyone, standard spelling wasn't

---

8 Kentish （英格兰东南部）肯特郡的
9 William Caxton 威廉 • 卡克斯顿（约1422—1491），英国第一位印刷商
10 printing press 印刷机

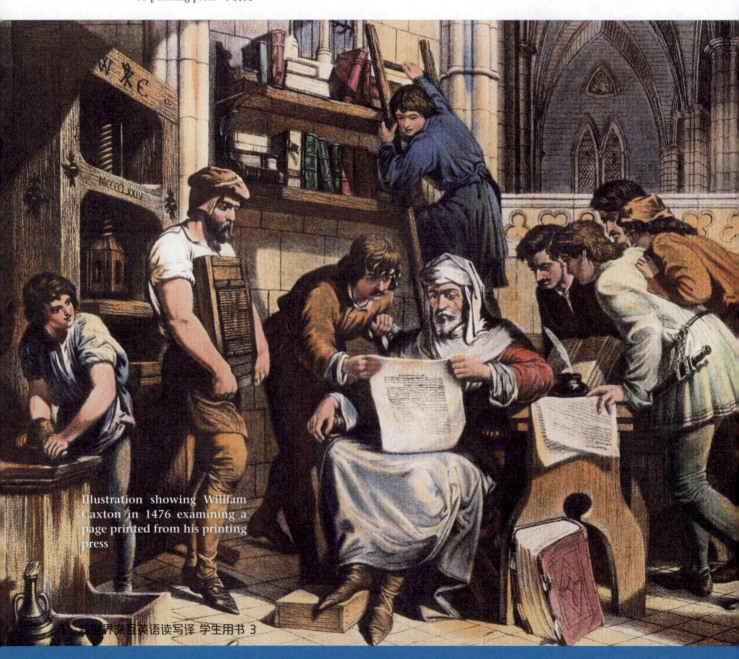

Illustration showing William Caxton in 1476 examining a page printed from his printing press

considered very important. As a matter of fact, the typesetters[11] in the 1500s made things even worse by being very careless about spelling. If a blank space needed to be filled in or a line was too long, they simply changed the spellings of words to make them fit. Moreover, many of the early printers in England were from Germany or Holland and didn't know English very well. If they didn't know the spelling of a word, they made one up! Different printers each had their favorite spellings, so one word might be spelled five or six different ways, depending on who printed the passage.

5   Throughout this period, names and words appear in many different forms. For instance, *where* can be found as *wher*, *whair*, *wair*, *wheare*, *were*, and so on. People were even very **liberal** about their names. More than 80 spellings of Shakespeare's name have been found, among them *Shagsspeare*, *Shakspeare*, and even *Shakestaffe*. Shakespeare himself didn't spell his name the same way in any two of his six known signatures—he even spelled his name two different ways in his will.

6   By the late 16th century and early 17th century, some progress had been made in standardizing spelling due to the work of various scholars. By then, however, English spelling was far from a simple phonetic system. For one thing, word pronunciations had changed too rapidly for a truly phonetic spelling to keep up. Also, English had borrowed from many languages and ended up having far too many sounds (more than 40) for the 26 letters in its Roman alphabet. By the time printing houses finally began to agree on standard spellings, many of these written forms were only a shadow of their spoken selves. In other words, spelling and pronunciation sometimes had little in common.

7   Finally, in 1755, Samuel Johnson[12] gave English its first great dictionary. His choice of spellings may not have always been the best or the easiest, but the book helped to make the spellings of most English words uniform. Eventually, people became aware of the need for "correct" spelling. Meanwhile, on the other side of the Atlantic, Noah Webster[13] was standardizing American English in his *An American Dictionary of the English Language* and *The American Spelling Book*. Although the British had been complaining about the messiness of English spelling for some time, it was the Americans, with their **fanaticism** for efficiency, who screamed the loudest. Webster not only favored a simplified, more phonetic spelling system, but also tried to persuade Congress to pass a law making the use of nonstandard spelling a punishable offense.

8   Mark Twain was of the same mind—but laziness figured into his opinion. He wasn't concerned so much with the difficulty of spelling words as with the trouble in writing them. He became a fan of the "phonographic alphabet", created by Isaac Pitman[14], the inventor of shorthand—a system in which symbols represent words, phrases, and letters. "To write the word 'laugh'," Twain wrote in *A Simplified Alphabet*,

---

11 typesetter（印刷）排字工人
12 Samuel Johnson 塞缪尔·约翰逊（1709—1784），英国辞典编纂家、作家、批评家和雄辩家
13 Noah Webster 诺亚·韦伯斯特（1758—1843），美国词典编纂家
14 Isaac Pitman 艾萨克·皮特曼（1813—1897），英国速记法的发明者

"the pen has to make fourteen strokes—no labor is saved to penman." But to write the same word in the phonographic alphabet, Twain continued, the pen had to make just three strokes. As much as Twain would have loved it, Pitman's phonographic alphabet never caught on.

9   Interest in reforming English spelling continued to **gain momentum** on both sides of the Atlantic. For a while, it seemed as if every famous writer and scholar had jumped on the spelling bandwagon. Spelling reform associations began to pop up everywhere. In 1876, the American Philological Association[15] called for the "urgent" adoption of 11 new spellings: *liv*, *tho*, *thru*, *wisht*, *catalog*, *definit*, *gard*, *giv*, *hav*, *infinit*, and *ar*. In the same year, the Spelling Reform Association was formed, followed three years later by a British version.

10   In 1906, the **philanthropist** Andrew Carnegie[16] gave $250,000 to help establish the Simplified Spelling Board. The board quickly issued a list of 300 words that were commonly spelled two ways, such as *ax* and *axe*, and called for using the simpler of the two. The board helped to gain acceptance for quite a few American spellings, including *catalog*, *demagog*, and *program*.

11   Eventually the Simplified Spelling Board **got carried away** with its work, calling for such spellings as *tuff*, *def*, *troble*, and *yu*. The call for simplified spelling quickly went out of fashion, particularly with the **onset** of World War I and the death of Andrew Carnegie. The movement never died out completely, however. Spelling reform continued to be an ongoing, if less dramatic, process, and many words have **shed** useless letters. *Deposite* has lost its *e*, as have *fossile* and *secretariate*. *Musick* and *physick* have dropped their needless *k*s, and *catalogue* and *dialogue* have shed their last two vowels.

12   As long as the world goes around, language will continue to change. New words will be added to English; spellings will be altered. But because people are most comfortable with the familiar, it's not likely that we'll ever see a major change in the way most words are spelled. Anyway, what would we do without the challenge of English spelling?

Vocabulary

Vocabulary in Context

A What are the meanings of the **bold** words or phrases? Circle the letter of the best answer.

1. The **merging** of the different languages gave birth to Old English.

   a. crossing **b.** confusion

   c. blending **d.** complication

2. By the 14th century, English, with its mix of languages, had **evolved** into what is called Middle English.

   a. improved **b.** appeared

   c. spread **d.** developed

---

15 American Philological Association (APA) 美国语文学协会，成立于1869年，后更名为古典研究协会
16 Andrew Carnegie 安德鲁·卡内基（1835—1919），美国工业家、慈善家

3. Even scholars were quite **indifferent to** matters of consistency in spelling and were known to spell the same word several different ways in a single sentence.

   a. uncaring about
   b. superior about
   c. unsocial about
   d. confused about

4. People were even **liberal** about the spelling of their names, using different spellings on the same page.

   a. receptive
   b. interested
   c. understanding
   d. free

5. Americans, with their **fanaticism** for efficiency, complained the most about the messiness of English spelling.

   a. spirit
   b. obsession
   c. excitement
   d. fascination

6. Interest in reforming English spelling continued to **gain momentum** on both sides of the Atlantic.

   a. be temporary
   b. become stable
   c. grow stronger
   d. get weak

7. The **philanthropist** Andrew Carnegie gave $250,000 to help establish the Simplified Spelling Board.

   a. person being an expert in language
   b. person actively helping others
   c. person famous for his or her written work
   d. person known for his or her wealth

8. The Spelling Board outlived its usefulness when it **got carried away with** its work.

   a. became overenthusiastic about
   b. was removed from
   c. got to continue
   d. became successful in

9. The call for simplified spelling went out of fashion with the **onset** of World War I.

   a. outcome
   b. tragedy
   c. end
   d. start

10. Many words **shed** useless letters.

    a. changed
    b. kept
    c. dropped
    d. added

B Answer these questions with complete sentences.

1. Who is a well-known **philanthropist**?

   _____

2. What were you doing when you last **got carried away**?

   _____

3. What animal **sheds** its skin?

   _____

4. What is a sign of **fanaticism** in a person?

   _____

5. What is one way in which transportation has **evolved** in the past 50 years?

_____

C Now write your own sentences. Use the following words or phrases in the sentences: **gain momentum**, **merging**, **liberal**, **indifferent**, and **onset**.

_____
_____
_____

Vocabulary Building

A Match the nouns in the box with the adjectives below, as they were used in the context of the reading. The first one is done for you. Then look back at the reading to check your answers, and add two more nouns that may be used with each adjective.

| change | language | offense | process | spelling | system |

1. official   _____language_____   _____   _____
2. standard   _____   _____   _____
3. phonetic   _____   _____   _____
4. punishable _____   _____   _____
5. ongoing   _____   _____   _____
6. major   _____   _____   _____

B Use the nouns and adjectives you listed in Exercise A to complete these sentences about English spelling.

1. Spelling reform continues to be a(n) _____ _____.

2. _____ _____ was introduced with the first dictionaries.

3. It is unlikely that there will be any _____ _____ in English spelling now.

4. Spelling did not represent the _____ _____ of English.

5. Middle English became the _____ _____ of Britain by the 14th century.

6. Webster wanted to make the use of nonstandard spelling a(n) _____ _____.

Reading Comprehension

A Circle the letter of the best answer.

1. The main idea of Paragraph 3 is that _____.

   a. by the time English became a written language, the influence of several languages and dialects had made spelling and pronunciation very inconsistent

   b. scholars didn't help the problem of spelling inconsistency, because they often spelled words several different ways

c. in Britain, English words had different spellings and pronunciations in different parts of the country

   d. by the 14th century, English had evolved into Middle English and was Britain's official language

2. Paragraph 12 is mainly concerned with _____.

   a. the work of the Simplified Spelling Board

   b. why the call for simplified spelling went out of fashion

   c. the many words that have been shortened by dropping useless letters

   d. the ongoing changes in the English language

3. The purpose which spelling reform associations served was _____.

   a. to simplify the spellings of many words

   b. to achieve major savings in labor in writing words

   c. to help Pitman's phonographic alphabet catch on

   d. to prevent writers and scholars from jumping on the spelling bandwagon

4. The reading implies that _____.

   a. conquering tribes forced the Britons to speak their languages

   b. English was a "pure" language before the 14th century

   c. the influence of other languages made English a rich but complicated language

   d. when Britain made English its official language, it stopped foreign words from entering the language and making it even more complicated

5. From the reading, it can be concluded that _____.

   a. scholars weren't much more educated than the masses

   b. until the first dictionaries were written, even educated people weren't overly concerned with the spelling of words

   c. the invention of the printing press didn't have a significant influence on the English language

   d. there was no real need for an English dictionary before Johnson wrote his in 1755

B Complete the summary below using the list of words in the box.

standardize	rectify	coincide	momentum	inconsistency
resorting	coherent	resolving	ongoing	liberal
missionary	intricate	messiness	philanthropists	phonetic

In the reading, the author points out the phenomenon of the **1.**_____ or chaos of English spelling, in other words, the disparity between English spelling and pronunciation, and explains about the **2.**_____ structure of English spelling. In history, the English language was influenced by the languages of invaders at least four times, only to exhibit the **3.**_____ between spelling and pronunciation. To make things worse, people, even scholars and printers, didn't care whether spelling was **4.**_____ with pronunciation.

Unit 1 Language   11

Another reason why spelling didn't **5.** _____ with pronunciation is that the evolution of pronunciation was much quicker than the development of genuinely **6.** _____ spelling. Later, lexicographers, writers, **7.** _____ and scholars tried to **8.** _____ English spelling by simplifying spelling or **9.** _____ to shorthand to save the labor of writing. Even though the spelling reform encountered many obstacles, English spelling has been naturally changing in a(n) **10.** _____ process.

Critical Thinking

Discuss these questions with your classmates.

1. Why do you think proposals to reform English spelling have not won support?
2. What are your special strategies for remembering difficult spellings in English?
3. What does a language tell us about the country and its people who speak it?
4. In some countries, people speak more than one language, even several different languages. What are the advantages or disadvantages of this?
5. Do you think the world should have a universal language? Why or why not?

Reading 2

Pre-Reading

Preparing for the Reading Topic

A Discuss these questions with your classmates.

1. What are some different ways that new words can get introduced into a language?

2. What are some words in the English language that are used to describe things that are very large?

3. What are some words that are used to describe things that are very small?

B What do you think are the origins of the following words? Match the word with its origin. Then use a dictionary to check your answers.

_____ 1. lilac   _____ 4. aquarium

_____ 2. zero   _____ 5. antique

_____ 3. video   _____ 6. malevolent

a. from a Latin word meaning "to see"

b. from a Latin word for "water"

c. from a Sanskrit word that meant "nothing" and "desert"

d. from a Greek word meaning "old"

e. from a Latin word for "bad"

f. from a Persian word meaning "of a bluish shade"

Key Vocabulary

As you read "Jumbo", pay attention to the following words and phrases and see if you can work out their meanings from the contexts.

affectionate	approximately
exhibited	legendary
sensation	thrilling
encountered	retired
customary	on display

"Jumbo"

The following reading comes from It's a Wonderful Word *by Albert Jack, published in Great Britain in 2011.*

1   Jumbo is a word we associate with anything on a huge scale. We talk of jumbo-sized packets of crisps or jumbo jets, and use it as an **affectionate** nickname for an elephant. And it is to a real-life elephant that we owe the expression.

2   The original Jumbo was a huge African bush elephant born in 1861 in the French Sudan, now Mali[1]. As a youngster, he was taken to the Jardin des Plantes[2] in Paris and

---

1 Mali 马里，非洲西部国家
2 Jardin des Plantes 巴黎植物园

A herd of African elephants in Etosha National Park, Namibia

exhibited there until 1865, before being transferred to London Zoo, where he became famous by giving rides to thousands of children. His keepers there called him Jumbo, borrowing the word from the Swahili[3] *jambe*, "chief". Jumbo was quite the **sensation** at a time when most people had never **encountered** a twelve-foot, seven-ton beast, let alone had the chance to ride on one.

3   Such was his popularity that, when the zoo announced he was up for sale in 1882, over 100,000 schoolchildren wrote to Queen Victoria[4] begging her not to allow him to leave. The old queen, with her **customary** consideration of her subjects, ignored

---
3 Swahili 斯瓦希里语，非洲东部作为通用语广泛使用的一种班图语
4 Queen Victoria 维多利亚女王（1819—1901），英国、爱尔兰女王（1837—1901）和印度女王（1876—1901）

them all and sold Jumbo for £10,000, **approximately** £4 million in today's money, to the **legendary** circus owner P. T. Barnum[5], producer of the "Greatest Show on Earth". To misquote Oscar Wilde[6] in reference to the queen: "If this is the way she treats her subjects [originally 'prisoner'—meaning himself, before being carted off to Reading Gaol[7]], she doesn't deserve to have any."

4   Jumbo embarked upon a three-year tour across America, **thrilling** the crowds wherever he went, but on a visit to Ontario[8] in 1885 he was hit by a steam train and died. Some reports of the time claimed he died saving the life of a young elephant called Tom Thumb, of which there is absolutely no evidence, but it didn't do the legend of the world's most famous animal any harm. Alas[9], his work didn't end there: the unscrupulous Barnum had his hide[10] stuffed and continued to tour with him for the next four years.

5   After Jumbo was finally **retired** in 1889, he spent almost a century **on display** at Tufts University[11] in Boston, Massachusetts, but a fire in 1975 destroyed the building and the great chief himself.

---

5 P. T. Barnum 菲尼亚斯·泰勒·巴纳姆（1810—1891），美国马戏团经理人
6 Oscar Wilde 奥斯卡·王尔德（1854—1900），爱尔兰剧作家、小说家、诗人和哲人
7 Reading Gaol 雷丁监狱，位于英格兰南部
8 Ontario 安大略，加拿大省名，省会为多伦多
9 alas 不幸的是
10 hide 兽皮
11 Tufts University 塔夫茨大学，位于美国马萨诸塞州波士顿

Painting of the original Jumbo

Vocabulary

A What are the meanings of the **bold** words or phrases? Circle the letter of the best answer.

1. We use *Jumbo* as an **affectionate** nickname for an elephant.
   - a. unkind
   - b. loving
   - c. unusual
   - d. silly or amusing

2. Jumbo was **exhibited** in Paris until 1865.
   - a. hidden away in a secret place
   - b. moved from one place to another
   - c. put in a special area
   - d. shown in public for people to see

3. Jumbo was a **sensation** at the time.
   - a. something that caused excited interest
   - b. something that caused a great fear
   - c. something that caused worry
   - d. something that caused arguments and conflict

4. Most people had never **encountered** a twelve-foot, seven-ton beast.
   - a. come across
   - b. discovered
   - c. been friends with
   - d. learned about

5. The old queen showed her **customary** consideration of her subjects.
   - a. odd
   - b. important
   - c. usual
   - d. unnecessary

6. The queen sold Jumbo for **approximately** 4 million pounds.
   - a. exactly
   - b. close to
   - c. all of
   - d. far from

7. Jumbo was sold to the **legendary** circus owner P.T. Barnum.
   - a. unknown
   - b. regal
   - c. famous
   - d. worthy

8. Jumbo toured across America, **thrilling** the crowds.
   - a. causing a feeling of deep fear
   - b. causing a feeling of excitement and pleasure
   - c. causing a feeling of deep anger
   - d. causing a feeling of great sadness

9. Jumbo was **retired** in 1889.
   - a. replaced
   - b. destroyed
   - c. thrown away
   - d. not used anymore

10. Jumbo's body spent almost a century **on display** in Boston.
    - a. being hidden from view
    - b. being used as an object of study
    - c. being made into a useful object
    - d. being put out for all to see

B Answer these questions with complete sentences.

1. What movie became an overnight **sensation** in the past year?

2. Who is a **legendary** figure in history that you admire?

3. Why are some performing animals **retired**?

4. What is something that is **exhibited** at a Natural History Museum?

5. What is a **thrilling** sport to watch?

C Now write your own sentences. Use the following words or phrases in the sentences: ***customary, on display, approximately, affectionate,*** and ***encountered***.

Reading Comprehension

A Circle the letter of the best answer.

1. Which of the following statements is a main idea of the reading?
    a. Jumbo gave rides to thousands of children at London Zoo.
    b. Over 100,000 schoolchildren wrote to the queen.
    c. Barnum had Jumbo's hide stuffed.
    d. Jumbo's work didn't end with his death.

2. Schoolchildren wrote to _____, begging her not to allow Jumbo to leave the country.
    a. Queen Elizabeth I   b. Queen Anne
    c. Queen Victoria   d. Queen Elizabeth II

3. Jumbo was killed during a visit to _____ in 1885.
    a. Ontario   b. London
    c. Boston   d. Mali

4. Which of the following statements is a fact mentioned in the reading?
    a. Jumbo didn't live the normal life of an American elephant.
    b. Oscar Wilde didn't think very highly of the Queen.
    c. In 1865, Jumbo was transferred to London Zoo.
    d. Although huge, Jumbo was a gentle elephant.

5. Which of the following statements can be inferred from the reading?

   a. As a youngster, Jumbo was exhibited in Paris.

   b. Queen Victoria didn't care much about the opinions of her subjects.

   c. Some people said Jumbo died saving a young elephant.

   d. Jumbo thrilled audiences wherever he went.

B Find information in the reading to answer these questions. Write the number of the paragraph where you find the answer. Discuss your answers with a partner.

1. Under what circumstances did Jumbo cause a sensation in London?
   _____
   _____

   Paragraph: _____

2. Why did so many schoolchildren plead with the British queen not to sell Jumbo to a circus?
   _____
   _____

   Paragraph: _____

3. What final heroic act was Jumbo reported to have carried out?
   _____
   _____

   Paragraph: _____

Critical Thinking

Discuss these questions with your classmates.

1. What English words have come into use in Chinese? What Chinese words have come into use in English? Why do you think some words are borrowed from another language and not changed in any way?

2. New words, such as "google", are being added to English all the time. How do you think these words are created? What are 10 other words that did not exist 25–50 years ago? If you could create a new word for something, what would it be and why?

3. What changes in society over time have led to the creation of new words? In what periods of history do you think new words were added at a faster pace? What changes in the past 50 years have had the greatest impact on the creation of new words?

4. The Inuit of Alaska have many words and phrases for snow and ice, while the Arabic language has many words for "sand". What does this tell us about language and our environment?

5. How do you think today's youth-oriented society affects our language? Do you think youth have always introduced new words to languages? Why or why not?

Writing

Writing Skills

The Process Essay

There are different types of *process essays*. However, the essential component in all process essays is chronological or time order.

- **A process essay can describe events in the order they occurred.** These are events that occurred over a period of time, such as a morning, a day, a childhood, or the duration of a war. A history or a biography usually describes events over a period of time.

- **A process essay can describe a technical process.** This type of essay describes processes such as how a computer works or how hair is transplanted or how chocolate is made. (This type of essay contains many verbs in the passive form.)

- **A process essay can be a "how-to" essay.** With this type of process essay, you tell someone how to do or make something. This type is used to discuss topics such as how to prepare a special dish or how to get a driver's license.

Thesis Statement for the Process Essay

- The *thesis statement for the process essay* can vary depending on which type of process is being described.

- The thesis statement for a process that is historical should name the process and indicate chronological order through words like *developed* or *evolved*.
   - EXAMPLE: Chinese is one of the world's oldest languages, and its written form, like that of most languages, **developed** from the pictograph.

- The thesis statement for a technical process should name the process and indicate that it involves a series of steps.
   - EXAMPLE: Hair transplantation is a fairly simple process. The main steps in the process of hair transplantation are removal of the desired number of hair transplants, removal of small plugs in the bald area, and insertion of the hair transplants.

- The thesis statement for a "how-to" essay is the same as the one for a technical process. It should name the process or item and indicate that it involves a number of steps.
   - EXAMPLE: Rescue breathing for a person who is unconscious involves a sequence of steps that must be followed carefully.

Organizing the Process Essay

- Deciding how to divide a process essay into paragraphs can be tricky. If you are writing a historical or narrative piece about a chronological process, divide your paragraphs by major time periods. However, if you are writing about how to do something, the following guidelines will help you.

- **Introduction.** Introduce the topic and explain why the process is performed, by whom it is performed, and in what situation it is performed. You may list the main steps of the process in the order they are performed.

- **Body Paragraphs.** Start to describe the process, introducing the first step in a topic sentence. You may at this point state the equipment and supplies needed for the process. Divide the process into three or four major steps. Each major step should be described in a body paragraph. For example, if you were describing a wedding ceremony in China, the first major step would be the preparations, the next would be the ceremony, and the last would be the reception or banquet.

- **Conclusion.** Summarize by restating the main steps and describing the result. The type of conclusion will depend on the type of process you are describing.

Time Expressions

Time may be indicated by a preposition with a date or historical period: *in 1920*, *by the 16th century*, *over the next 10 years*, or other time expressions. The following are some prepositions, conjunctions or adverbs commonly used with time.

- *During* indicates the duration of the activity from beginning to end, usually without stating the length of time.

    EXAMPLE: **During** her time at college, she performed remarkably.

- *For* indicates the length of time or an appointed time.

    EXAMPLES: I waited **for** an hour.
    My appointment was **for** three o'clock.

- *Since* indicates a period of time from its beginning to the present.

    EXAMPLE: He has been living there **since** 1920. (He is still there.)

- Other time prepositions, time conjunctions or time adverbs indicate when or how long: *as*, *in*, *on*, *to*, *till*, *up to*, *upon*, *as early as*, *as soon as*, *from/to*, and *as late as*.

    EXAMPLES: The process should be completed **in** three hours.
    The class will have a test **on** Friday.
    He worked **till** ten o'clock.
    She spends **up to** three hours every day rehearsing.
    She woke up **as soon as** it was daylight.
    Cook the beans **from** 25 **to** 35 minutes.

- Dependent clauses can be introduced by prepositions or conjunctions (*after*, *before*, *until*, *when*, *while*).

    EXAMPLES: **After** (or **when**) you have made a rough draft, start revising your work.

    Before starting on the second draft, make sure that your details support your topic sentences.

    Don't forget to look up the spelling of words you are unsure of **when** you are editing.

    Do not be distracted **while** you are editing each sentence.

- Other useful words that indicate a sequence in a process are ordinal numbers (*first*, *second*, *third*) and interrupters (*next*, *then*, *later*, *simultaneously*, *eventually*). The expressions **previous to**, **prior to**, and **just before** place an action before another action.

    EXAMPLES: **Prior to** writing your research, make sure you have all the information at hand.

    Next, revise your draft.

Exercise

Complete the paragraphs below using the time words and phrases in the box. Each choice can be used only once.

after	for	in 1542	later	then	when
during	in 1499	in 1637	still	until	while

The first European to discover the Amazon River was Spanish explorer Vicente Pinzón

1. _____. He had been on Columbus's first voyage seven years earlier and was

The Amazon River seen from the air near Iquitos, Peru

2. _____ determined to find a route to the Orient. 3. _____ he sailed into the mouth of the Amazon and looked at the mighty river ahead of him, he thought he had gone around the world and hit the Ganges River in India. He stopped at some islands in the mouth of the river and 4. _____ sailed on.

Forty-three years 5. _____ , 6. _____ , Francisco de Orellana became the first European to travel the entire river, although that was not what he set out to do at all. 7. _____ a Spanish expedition became stranded in the jungles of Eastern Peru, Orellana was sent down the Napo River to find food. But starvation, sickness, and Indian attacks took place, and Orellana couldn't get back upriver. Instead, he followed tributaries to the Amazon, and 8. _____ 16 months of incredible hardships, he and what was left of his party made it all the way to the sea.

In 1561, the notorious Lope de Aguirre traveled the Amazon 9. _____ on the run from Spanish troops. He left a trail of death and destruction throughout the Amazon, all the way to the sea.

No one traveled the entire river 10. _____ another 76 years, 11. _____ a Portuguese captain, Pedro Teixeira, became the first to complete an upriver "ascent" 12. _____ .

Writing Practice

Write an Essay

Choose one of the following topics to write a process essay.

1. How you recovered from an illness or accident
2. Learning a foreign language
3. The sequence of steps for a ceremony in China (for example, a wedding)

Pre-Write

A Work with a partner and think about how you might divide your process essay into three or four parts.

B Work on a thesis statement for your essay.

Organize Your Ideas

A Write your thesis statement.

B Divide your steps into three or four paragraphs.

C Provide details of each step in the paragraphs.

D Make a detailed outline, showing what will be in the Introduction, Body, and Conclusion.

Write a Rough Draft

Using your detailed outline and any notes you made in Pre-Write, write a rough draft of your essay.

Revise Your Rough Draft

Check the thesis statement, unity, development, coherence and purpose of your rough draft.

Edit Your Essay

Work with a partner or your teacher to edit your essay. Check the spelling, punctuation, vocabulary, and grammar.

Write Your Final Copy

After you edit your essay, you can write your final copy.

Translation

A Translate the following passage into English.

现行的简体字主要是在1956年审订通过的，旨在提高大众的读写能力。其简化原则包括"述而不作""约定俗成，稳步前进"。其中多数简体字选自历代的草书（cursive script），早在南北朝的碑刻（tablet inscription）上就已出现。汉字简化改革的呼声由来已久，但我们不提倡"过度简化"，必须保持汉字形体的相对稳定性。其他使用汉字的国家，也使用简体字。新加坡和马来西亚和我们使用同一套简体字，泰国发行了简繁体字对照表，日本和韩国的简体汉字与中国的也有很多相同之处。

B Translate the following passage into Chinese.

As much as Noah Webster helped standardize many American phonetic spellings, attempts to reform the spelling of English have usually met with failure. The spelling of English is constantly and naturally evolving and there cannot be a one-to-one sound-to-spelling correspondence. What makes English spelling and pronunciation inconsistent is not merely the shortage of English letters, but mainly the use of many different letters or letter combinations for the same sound, and the use of identical letters or letter sequences for spelling different sounds. Moreover, English often makes no attempt to localize the foreign spellings to conform to English spelling standards. There are some other reasons for making English spelling irregular. For instance, there was a period when people altered the spelling of a small number of words out of consideration for the origins of the words; commercials have also had an effect on English spelling; the spellings of personal names have also been a source of spelling innovations.

Weaving It Together

Unit Project

Choose one of the following topics and give a presentation on the process of the topic to your classmates.

1. How you recovered from an illness or accident
2. Learning a foreign language
3. The sequence of steps for a ceremony in China (for example, a wedding)

Searching the Internet

A Search the Internet for information about the American Spelling Reform Movement. Find answers to these questions:

1. Who started the spelling reform movement in American English?
2. What did he or she accomplish with this reform?
3. Was this reform successful? Why or why not?
4. What are some words that are spelled differently in American and British English?

B Search the Internet for information on one of the following processes. Share the information with your classmates.

- How the education system works (in China or the United States)
- How the digestive system works
- How a holiday is celebrated (in China or the United States)
- How babies learn to talk
- How a volcano explodes

C You may use your research later to write a process essay.

What Do You Think Now?

Refer to the very beginning of this unit. Do you know the answers now? Circle the best answer.

1. English (was/wasn't) a mix of five languages at one time.
2. Shakespeare (spelled/didn't spell) his name in different ways all the time.
3. New words (are/are not) being added to languages all the time.
4. All English words (have/don't have) the same origin.

Broadening Your Horizon

A Brief History of English Spelling Reform

The way we spell words seems integral to our identity. But spelling is neither fixed nor permanent, and we have a long history of attempts to reform it—some more successful than others.

How to Talk Like a Pilgrim
A Short Glossary of 17th-Century Terms and Phrases

When the Mayflower sailed across the Atlantic in 1620, its passengers brought with them an English language that was still in the process of evolving into its modern form. The first single-language English dictionary, Robert Cawdrey's 3,000-word *Table Alphabeticall*, had been published just 16 years earlier, and the language still lacked firm grammatical rules.

English Is Not Normal

No, English isn't uniquely vibrant or mighty or adaptable. But it really is weirder than pretty much every other language.

UNIT 2 Hygiene

Young men bathe in the Tuichi River in Madidi National Park, Bolivia.

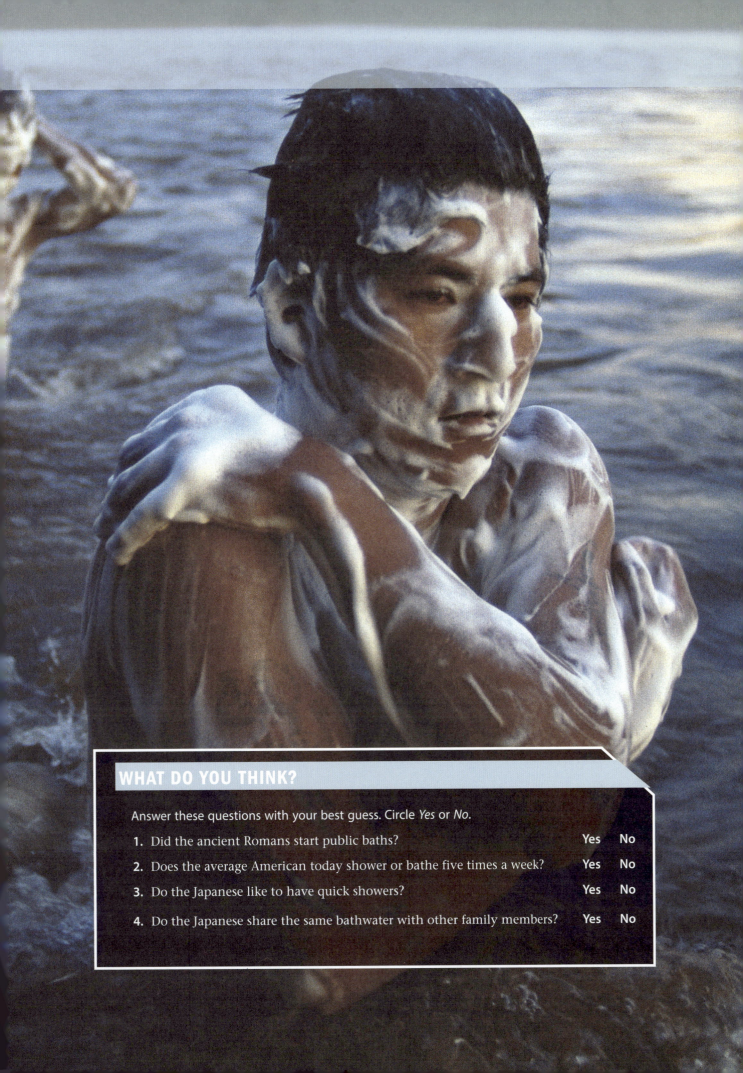

WHAT DO YOU THINK?

Answer these questions with your best guess. Circle *Yes* or *No*.

1. Did the ancient Romans start public baths? Yes No
2. Does the average American today shower or bathe five times a week? Yes No
3. Do the Japanese like to have quick showers? Yes No
4. Do the Japanese share the same bathwater with other family members? Yes No

Reading 1

Pre-Reading

Preparing for the Reading Topic

A Discuss these questions with your classmates.

1. Look at this photo of a traditional Iranian public bathhouse built in the sixteenth century. Does Chinese culture have similar public bathhouses? Describe them.

2. What is your opinion of public baths? Why do you think they are important in some cultures?

3. In addition to getting clean, what are some other reasons for taking a bath?

B Decide if the following statements are True (*T*) or False (*F*). Then compare your answers with those of your classmates.

_____ 1. The ancient Romans did not place much emphasis on personal cleanliness.

_____ 2. The ancient Greeks used oil instead of soap to clean themselves.

_____ 3. Sweat baths or *hammams* started in Europe.

_____ 4. During the Middle Ages in Europe, people bathed when they were baptized and seldom after that.

_____ 5. After 1800, bathing became a good thing in North America.

The Sultan Amir Ahmad Bathhouse in Kashan, Iran, is a traditional Iranian public bathhouse that was originally constructed in the sixteenth century.

Key Vocabulary

As you read "How Clean Is Clean?", pay attention to the following words and phrases and see if you can work out their meanings from the contexts.

virtue	infested with
anointment with	rampant
indulged in	grave
repressed	overtones
boasted	retreats

How Clean Is Clean?

1   **C**leanliness is considered a **virtue**, but just what does it mean to be clean? As most of us have had the unpleasant occasion to discover, one person's definition can be quite different from another's. From Istanbul[1] to Indianapolis[2], people have their own ways of keeping clean and their own reasons for doing so.

2   Cleanliness has had a long and varied history with mixed reviews. Sometimes it's popular; sometimes it's not. Throughout the ages, personal cleanliness has been greatly

---

1 Istanbul 伊斯坦布尔，土耳其城市
2 Indianapolis 印第安纳波利斯，美国印第安纳州首府

influenced by religion, culture, and technology. Moreover, bathing has served many functions in addition to hygiene. Baths are also places for social gathering, mental and physical relaxation, and medicinal treatment. Archaeological evidence suggests that bathing is as old as the first civilizations. Soap-like material has been found in clay jars of Babylonian origin, dating back to about 2800 BCE[3]. One of the first known bathtubs came from Minoan Crete[4], and a pretty sophisticated plumbing system of clay pipes is known to have existed in the great palace of King Minos[5], built in 1700 BCE. The ancient Egyptians didn't have such plumbing expertise, but are known to have had a positive attitude toward hygiene. They washed with soapy material made of animal and vegetable oils and salts and sat in a shallow kind of bath while attendants poured water over them.

3 The Greeks prized cleanliness, although they didn't use soap. Instead, they rubbed oil and ashes on their bodies, scrubbed with blocks of rocks or sand, and scraped themselves clean with a curved metal instrument. A dip in the water and **anointment with** olive oil followed. They were no doubt clean, but how would they smell if we followed them down the street today?

4 There were public Grecian baths as well as private ones, but they didn't serve the social purpose of the Roman baths. It seems that no one in history has **indulged in** bathing the way the Romans did. Nearly a dozen large and magnificent public bathhouses dotted the city, and many hundreds of private baths were found in homes. Emperor Caracalla[6]'s bath could accommodate 1,600 bathers at a time. Emperor Diocletian[7] entertained crowds of more than 3,000 in the marble splendor of his bath, finished in 305 CE[8]. Apparently the Romans had lots of time on their hands, because bathing was not just an exercise; it was an event. First, a bather entered a warm room to sweat and to engage in lengthy conversations. Fine oils and sand were used to cleanse the body. Next came a hot room where the bather would be treated to even more sweating, splashing with water, more oils and scraping, and yet more talk. Finally, the Romans concluded the process by plunging into a cool and refreshing pool. In the early years of the baths, men and women had separate areas, but eventually the sexes mixed and the baths lost their virtuous purpose.

5 So corrupt were Roman society and its baths that the fathers of the early Christian church[9] discouraged bathing. The hygienic practices of the Greeks and Romans were **repressed** to such an extent that Europe during the Middle Ages[10] has been said to have gone a thousand years without a bath. Queen Isabella of Castile[11] **boasted** that she had bathed only twice in her life—at birth and before her marriage. Religion

---

3 BCE 公元前，纪年法，以相传的耶稣基督诞生年即公元元年作为历史算起，公元前指公元元年之前

4 Minoan Crete 克里特文明，公元前3000—前1100，也称为米诺斯文明或迈诺安文明，是爱琴海地区的古代文明，出现于古希腊，主要集中在克里特岛

5 King Minos 米诺斯王，希腊神话中宙斯与欧罗巴之子，克里特之王

6 Emperor Caracalla 罗马皇帝卡拉卡拉（188—217）

7 Emperor Diocletian 罗马皇帝戴克里先（245—313）

8 CE 公元，纪年法，以相传的耶稣基督诞生年即公元元年作为历史算起

9 Christian church 基督教会，基督教徒对基督教组织的习惯称呼

10 the Middle Ages 中世纪（约476—1453），欧洲历史上的一个时代

11 Queen Isabella of Castile 卡斯蒂利亚女王伊莎贝拉（1451—1504），为统一的西班牙奠定了基础，赞助哥伦布去往西印度群岛的远航，建立了异端裁判所

wasn't the only reason why Europeans didn't bathe. Although the royal and wealthy sometimes indulged, commoners found bathing virtually impossible. With no running water, polluted rivers, and soap taxed as a luxury item, the ordinary citizen had little opportunity to bathe. As a result, people lived in filth, clothing was **infested with** vermin, and disease was **rampant**.

6   Early Americans, being of European origin, brought their dirty habits with them. By the 1800s, however, both Europeans and Americans were reforming their ways. As it became known that filth led to disease, governments began to improve sanitation standards. Wash houses were built, and bathing became a good thing again. In the United States, tubs, water heaters, and good indoor plumbing put bathing within the reach of ordinary citizens. They like it so much that today the average American claims to shower or bathe more than seven times a week.

7   In North America, clean means not only free of dirt, but free of odor as well—or, rather, human odors, because millions of dollars are spent each year on powders and perfumes that cover up any natural smells that might slip by. As any deodorant ad will tell you, to have body odor (B.O.) is a **grave** social offense.

8   In many Middle Eastern countries, cleanliness has religious **overtones** that link spiritual and physical purification. The Jewish people have many religious laws relating to hygiene, both personal and in the preparation of food. Muslims[12], too, live by some very strict rules related to cleanliness. For example, they are required to wash certain parts of their bodies, such as their feet and hands, before they pray. Since the time of Mohammed[13], sweat baths, or *hammams*[14], have been recommended. They serve not only as places for cleansing but also as **retreats** and opportunities for socializing. In the Middle Ages, the Crusaders[15], who enjoyed hammams, brought the idea of the public bath back to Europe with them and introduced the use of thermal baths as therapy for a variety of ills.

9   For many Middle Easterners, baths are a sort of ritual, a major affair that takes longer than an hour. Bathing begins with a steam, followed by rubbing the body with a hard towel, then soaping and rinsing. People usually want to lie down after a bath. Since it takes so long and is so exhausting, they indulge in these baths once a week.

10 Asian cultures are very strict and ritualistic about their cleanliness. The Japanese in particular are known for their personal hygiene, which extends from removing their shoes and putting on special slippers before entering any house or building to extensive washing before meals.

11 It is logical to conclude that cleanliness has many different meanings and is judged by a variety of standards. *Clean* means pure, in a religious sense, as well as clean of body. For some, it means being "squeaky clean" and smelling like roses. For others, a more "natural" state is acceptable. Whether it means washing one's hands and face or a head-to-toe scrubbing, cleanliness is a cultural practice, with enough stories and emotions behind it to make a real soap opera.

---

12 Muslim 穆斯林，伊斯兰教信徒
13 Mohammed 穆罕默德（570—632），政治家、宗教领袖，伊斯兰教的创复兴者
14 hammam 土耳其浴场
15 the Crusaders 十字军战士（1096—1291），在罗马天主教教皇的准许下，由西欧的封建领主和骑士对地中海东岸的国家发动的一系列宗教性军事行动的参战者

Vocabulary

Vocabulary in Context

A What are the meanings of the **bold** words or phrases? Circle the letter of the best answer.

1. For most people today, cleanliness is a **virtue**.
   - **a.** practical thing
   - **b.** natural thing
   - **c.** unimportant quality
   - **d.** good quality

2. A dip in the water and **anointment with** olive oil followed.
   - **a.** a rub with
   - **b.** an application of
   - **c.** a soak in
   - **d.** a wash with

3. No one in history **indulged in** bathing the way the Romans did.
   - **a.** pleased themselves by
   - **b.** made rules against
   - **c.** talked and wrote about
   - **d.** had the patience for

4. The hygienic practices of the Greeks and Romans were **repressed**.
   - **a.** encouraged
   - **b.** defined
   - **c.** held back
   - **d.** debated

5. Queen Isabella **boasted** that she had bathed only twice in her life.
   - **a.** said proudly
   - **b.** argued often
   - **c.** expressed quickly
   - **d.** denied strongly

6. The clothing of commoners was often **infested with** vermin.
   - **a.** free of
   - **b.** decorated with
   - **c.** made by
   - **d.** full of

7. Disease was **rampant**.
   - **a.** not commonly found
   - **b.** easily controlled
   - **c.** avoided at all cost
   - **d.** spread everywhere

8. In North America, body odor is a **grave** social offense.
   - **a.** serious
   - **b.** harmful
   - **c.** rare
   - **d.** frequent

9. In many Middle Eastern countries, cleanliness has religious **overtones**.
   - **a.** rituals
   - **b.** meanings
   - **c.** controls
   - **d.** results

10. Sweat baths also served as **retreats**.
    - **a.** locations for parties
    - **b.** opportunities to get work accomplished
    - **c.** places to get away and rest
    - **d.** areas in which to exercise

B Answer these questions with complete sentences.

1. What food do you like to **indulge in**?

2. What is a **grave** offense to someone in China?
   _____

3. When would people go to **retreats**?
   _____

4. What is your greatest **virtue**?
   _____

5. What city or area of a city is **rampant** with crime?
   _____

C Now write your own sentences. Use the following words or phrases in the sentences: ***anointment with**, **repressed**, **boasted**, **infested with**,* and ***overtones**.*

_____
_____
_____

Vocabulary Building

A Match the nouns in the box with the adjectives below, as they were used in the context of the reading. The first one is done for you. Then look back at the reading to check your answers, and add two more nouns that may be used with each adjective.

evidence	hygiene	offense	relaxation	reviews	treatment

1. mixed — _reviews_ — _____ — _____
2. mental — _____ — _____ — _____
3. medicinal — _____ — _____ — _____
4. archaeological — _____ — _____ — _____
5. social — _____ — _____ — _____
6. personal — _____ — _____ — _____

B Use the nouns and adjectives you listed in Exercise A to complete these sentences about cleanliness.

1. Ruins of many ancient civilizations show _____ _____ of baths.

2. Bathing is a form of _____ _____.

3. If you are sick, bathing can be a form of _____ _____.

4. Throughout history, the popularity of bathing has changed; it has had _____ _____.

5. If your body smells, it can be a(n) _____ _____.

6. _____ _____ is more important in some cultures than in others.

Reading Comprehension

A Circle the letter of the best answer.

1. The main idea of Paragraph 2 is that _____.
   a. bathing has many different functions in society besides that of cleansing the body
   b. indoor plumbing was achieved by the Minoans in Crete almost 4,000 years ago
   c. the Egyptians made up for their lack of sophisticated plumbing by having servants pour water over them while they bathed
   d. cleansing of the body has been done for thousands of years in many different ways and for many different reasons

2. Paragraph 8 is mainly concerned with _____.
   a. crusaders bringing the idea of public baths to Europe
   b. religious laws connected with cleanliness in the Middle East
   c. the importance of sweat baths in some countries
   d. the use of baths as a treatment for illness

3. During the Middle Ages, besides religion, other reasons why Europeans didn't bathe were _____.
   a. that there wasn't enough water, rivers were polluted, and soap was a luxury
   b. that there was no running water, rivers were dirty, and soap-like material was heavily taxed
   c. that water was polluted, soap was expensive and there was no tap water
   d. that there was insufficient clean water, too much ash, and expensive soap

4. The reading implies that _____.
   a. only the most advanced societies recognized the importance of cleanliness
   b. cleanliness can mean only one thing: a body free from dirt and odors
   c. soap and bathtubs have not always been necessary for cleanliness
   d. little evidence exists regarding the cleanliness habits of early civilizations

5. From the reading, it can be concluded that _____.
   a. religion has always had a detrimental effect on society's personal cleanliness
   b. over the ages some societies have valued personal cleanliness more than others
   c. during the Middle Ages, Europeans had no need to be concerned with personal cleanliness
   d. technology has had little effect on Americans' bathing habits

B Complete the summary below using the list of words in the box.

technology	enhance	presents	evidence	overtones
ritual	various	opposed	identical	coincidence
addicted	endorse	economy	attached	certificate

In the reading, the author 1. _____ the bathing history with the advance of personal cleanliness, and summarizes that cleanliness that has many different meanings is judged by 2. _____ standards, and influenced by religion, culture, and 3. _____ .

Archaeologists found **4.** _____ to confirm the bathing activities of people in many early ancient civilizations. The Greeks **5.** _____ importance to cleanliness. The Romans were **6.** _____ to bathing. Nevertheless, during the Middle Ages, the fathers of the early Christian church **7.** _____ bathing. By the 1800s, European and American governments began to **8.** _____ sanitation standards. In many Middle Eastern countries, cleanliness has religious **9.** _____ that are related to the pure state of mind and body. For many people from the Middle East, baths are a ritual activity. In the end, the author mentions Asian cultures take a serious attitude toward cleanliness, which is related to a sort of **10.** _____ .

Critical Thinking

Discuss these questions with your classmates.

1. How is body odor regarded in China and in other countries?
2. How important are grooming activities such as brushing your teeth or combing your hair?
3. How do you think hygiene and cleanliness became intertwined with religion? What purposes did hygiene and cleanliness serve? Have they been a benefit to humanity?
4. Why do you think cleansing rituals are important to people? What purposes do they serve?
5. How is modern life changing our knowledge and habits related to cleansing?

Boys wash their hands in Mali, West Africa.

Reading 2

Pre-Reading

Preparing for the Reading Topic

A Discuss these questions with your classmates.

1. What are some objects that people have in their bathing areas?

2. Why might a person prefer a long bath to a quick shower?

3. How does soaking in hot water affect a person's mind and body?

B Number the following actions in the order in which you think they are carried out. Then explain the purpose of each of these actions during bathing. Then after you have read "Bathing Japanese Style", review your answers.

_____ washing

_____ soaking

_____ rinsing

_____ scrubbing

_____ shampooing

Key Vocabulary

As you read "Bathing Japanese Style", pay attention to the following words and see if you can work out their meanings from the contexts.

soul	soaking
conveys	tingling
indulgent	scrubbed
efficiency	vigorously
ritual	accumulated

A public bathhouse in the resort town of Kurokawa Onsen in Kumamoto Prefecture, Japan

Bathing Japanese Style

The following passage is from The Japanese Bath *by Bruce Smith, published by Gibbs Smith in 2012.*

1. In the West, a bath is a place where one goes to cleanse the body; in Japan, it is where one goes to cleanse the **soul**. In America, the idea of getting in a tub to soak **conveys** either a bubble-filled luxury, an extravagant and **indulgent** alternative to the speed and **efficiency** of the shower, or a once-a-week pioneer-style necessity of avoiding body odor. When one bathes in Japan, it is about much more than cleanliness, though cleanliness is important. It is about family and community, the washing of each other's backs before bathing; about time to be alone and contemplative—time to watch the moon rise above the garden. The idea of taking time and care with one's bath in Japan is as important as taking time and care with cooking and serving dinner. Unlike America, where speed and efficiency are valued (and in many states, the idea of water

conservation), the Japanese make bathing a **ritual**—a prescribed order of rinsing, washing, and **soaking** that is passed down from one generation to the next, becoming an integral part of the society at large.

2   Japanese bathing is basically made up of four steps. First, after taking off one's clothes in the *datsuiba*[1], the bather steps into the washing area next to the bathtub and sits down on a small stool. It is usual here to dip one's hand into the hot water to check the temperature. Since the entire area is waterproof, one picks up a wooden bucket (unfortunately sometimes today it is made of plastic) and scoops hot water from the tub, pouring it over the shoulders. This is repeated several times, rinsing off the dirt from the entire body. Rinsing is accomplished rather quickly, the point being twofold: to clean off the dirt from one's body before entering the hot water that is to be shared by others and to accustom the body to the temperature of the bathwater.

3   Now that the body is ready for soaking, the bather climbs over the edge of the bathtub and slowly descends into the bath. If the bathwater is too hot, cold water from the faucet can be added—though traditionally the Japanese bath is hotter than baths taken in America, usually tending to be about 110 degrees (43.33 degrees Celsius). One slowly sinks into the water, and after a while, the body becomes used to the water, feeling gradually as though the heat has penetrated to its core. The **tingling** sensation disappears and changes into a mildly dull pleasant feeling. Usually this is the sign that the body is ready to be **scrubbed**. In winter, the first soaking can take up to ten minutes; in summer, it can be as short as three minutes.

4   Feeling somewhat heavy, as if one has been cooked, the bather gets out of the tub and sits down on the stool again. This time he or she gets a bucketful of water from the faucet. Rubbing soap onto a loofah, washcloth, or sponge, he or she completely rubs him or herself all over from head to toe. While still sitting down, the shampooing begins, and it is not unusual at this point for another family member to come in and help scrub the bather's back. The feeling is that now one has been cooked, it is time to **vigorously** scrub—to get every possible inch of dead skin and dirt scraped off the body. Most Japanese remain seated while soaping the body, taking care not to splash any soap scum into the tub water, and depending on mood, this scrubbing can take as long as ten to fifteen minutes.

5   The bather completely rinses off the soapsuds, then rinses once again. At this point, he or she is ready for the last soaking. Since the body is already warmed this time, it is easier to descend into clean water. The body feels smooth and soft after the vigorous scrubbing, and the muscles and nerves begin unwinding from **accumulated** tensions of the day. After this last soak, one might take a cold shower or simply splash some cold water over the shoulders. In the *datsuiba*, the bather dries off and puts on a *yukata* or comfortable clothing. Finally, the Japanese bath is finished and the rest of the evening awaits.

6   Taking a short bath is looked down upon—in Japan it is taking a *Karasu no gyozui*, or raven's bath, with the implication that it is done hastily and without care. The Japanese put the American shower into this category. Bathing is to be done with care, taking time and pleasure, and should be valued as a prescribed part of one's daily routine.

---

1 *datsuiba* 更衣室

Vocabulary

A What are the meanings of the **bold** words? Circle the letter of the best answer.

1. A Japanese bath is where one goes to cleanse the **soul**.
   - a. physical part of a person
   - b. thoughts of a person
   - c. spirit in a person
   - d. feelings of a person

2. In America, getting in a tub to soak **conveys** a bubble-filled luxury.
   - a. communicates a thought about
   - b. reveals a secret about
   - c. controls feelings about
   - d. makes one have doubts about

3. In America, soaking in a tub is an **indulgent** alternative to a shower.
   - a. allowing oneself a special pleasure
   - b. acting in a practical way
   - c. not getting what one wants
   - d. being strict in one's behavior

4. In America, soaking in a tub is an indulgent alternative to the **efficiency** of a shower.
   - a. state of being done in a slow and leisurely manner
   - b. state of being done according to one's normal habits
   - c. state of being done in the easiest way possible
   - d. state of being done quickly and without waste

5. The Japanese make bathing a **ritual**.
   - a. strange and unusual behavior
   - b. act repeatedly done the same way
   - c. new manner of doing things
   - d. way of acting in accordance with the law

6. The order of rinsing, washing, and **soaking** are passed down from one generation to the next.
   - a. taking something in and out of a liquid repeatedly
   - b. remaining in a liquid for a length of time
   - c. pulling out of a liquid rapidly
   - d. throwing into a liquid quickly

7. The **tingling** sensation disappears.
   - a. feeling a wave of heat in the body
   - b. feeling a sharp sensation of pain
   - c. feeling a prickly sensation on the skin
   - d. having bumps on the skin from being cold

8. This is a sign that the body is ready to be **scrubbed**.
   - a. pressed gently with hands to relieve aches
   - b. scratched lightly to stop itching
   - c. rubbed hard to cleanse
   - d. dried off with a towel

9. It is time to **vigorously** scrub.
   - a. thoroughly
   - b. forcefully
   - c. quickly
   - d. gently

10. Muscles and nerves begin unwinding from **accumulated** tensions.
    - a. collected
    - b. stored
    - c. created
    - d. unwanted

B Answer these questions with complete sentences.

1. What gives you a **tingling** sensation?
   _____

2. What have you **accumulated** over time?
   _____

3. What is one **ritual** you have in your life?
   _____

4. What task do you do with **efficiency**?
   _____

5. What is an **indulgent** behavior of yours?
   _____

C Now write your own sentences. Use the following words in the sentences: *vigorously*, *soul*, *soaking*, *scrubbed*, and *conveys*.

_____
_____
_____

Reading Comprehension

A Circle the letter of the best answer.

1. Which of the following statements is the main idea of the reading?

   a. In America, speed and efficiency are valued.

   b. In Japan, a bath is a place to cleanse the soul.

   c. Japanese bathing is about cleanliness and something more than cleanliness.

   d. The Japanese make bathing a ritual.

2. The Japanese have a prescribed order of rinsing, washing, and _____.

   a. splashing   b. rubbing

   c. scrubbing   d. soaking

3. After the last soak, a bather might take a cold shower or _____.

   a. rinse once again

   b. simply splash some cold water over the shoulders

   c. dry off and put on a yukata or comfortable clothing

   d. soap the body

4. Which of the following statements is a fact mentioned in the reading?

   a. Bathing in America doesn't have the same meaning and importance as in Japan.

   b. The Japanese bather takes the time to watch the moon rise over the garden.

- c. The Japanese are thoughtful of other bathers in the communal bath.
- d. In Japan, the bathing ritual changes somewhat with the seasons.

5. Which of the following statements can be inferred from the reading?
    - a. Though soaking in the Japanese bath can be long, rinsing is accomplished quickly.
    - b. In a Japanese bath, a family member helps with scrubbing the bather's back.
    - c. Soaking in hot water gives the body a dull, pleasant feeling.
    - d. Bathing is a form of relaxation at the end of the Japanese day.

B Find information in the reading to answer these questions. Note the number of the paragraph where you find the answer. Discuss your answers with a partner.

1. What is the sign that the body is ready to be scrubbed in Japanese bathing?

   Paragraph: _____

2. In Japanese bathing, after the vigorous scrubbing, what do the bathers feel?

   Paragraph: _____

3. What does "taking a raven's bath" imply?

   Paragraph: _____

Critical Thinking

Discuss these questions with your classmates.

1. Many Americans think long baths are a luxury. Why do you think this is? Why is the American lifestyle not suited to the Japanese bathing ritual?
2. What are your bathing habits? Do you prefer a long soak or a "raven's bath"? Why?
3. What are the bathing rituals or habits in China? Do you think bathing practices in China will change in the future? Why or why not?
4. How might the climate and environment in which people live affect their bathing habits?
5. Besides bathing, what are some other aspects of personal hygiene? Why is personal hygiene important to a person, family, and society in general?

Writing Skills

Pre-Writing Techniques

Before starting to write on a specific topic, it is important to develop some ideas. In the sections below, you will learn a number of strategies for generating ideas: brainstorming, clustering, and freewriting. These techniques are useful when you first start thinking about your topic and at other times when you find you have nothing to say about a topic.

Brainstorming

- To get ideas and stimulate your thoughts, you can use the strategy of *brainstorming*. You can brainstorm alone or with a group.

- Here are some guidelines to follow when brainstorming.
    - Give yourself or the group a limited amount of time.
    - Write down the word or phrase you need to get ideas about.
    - Write down all the ideas that come to mind. Do not organize your ideas in any way.
    - When your time is up, look over the ideas to see if any can be grouped together.

- The following is an example of the ideas that came up in a brainstorming session on the subject of video games for children. You will see that in this brainstorm, the writer found more negative than positive points to write down, so the writer might want to write about the negative sides of video games.

Video Games

addictive	*time-consuming*	*fun*
bad for eyes	*expensive*	*too violent*
more exciting than TV		*take time away from homework*

Exercise 1

A writer has started brainstorming on the topic of *home cleanliness*. Add to the ideas below. Then look at all the words and phrases and determine what you would write about.

Home Cleanliness

a lot of work	*less toxins*	*cleaner indoor air*
_____	_____	_____
_____	_____	_____

Clustering

- *Clustering* is another way of generating ideas. To cluster, you make a visual plan of the connections among your ideas.

- Use the following steps for clustering.
    1. Write your topic in the center of your paper and circle it.
    2. Write an idea related to the topic, circle that idea, and from it draw a line back to the topic. Keep writing down ideas, making circles around them, and connecting them back to the ideas they came from.
    3. When you have no more ideas, look at your clusters and decide which ideas seem most important.

- The following is an example of the ideas that came up in clustering on the subject of hot tubs. Using this diagram, the writer could then easily develop an essay on the pros and cons of hot tubs.

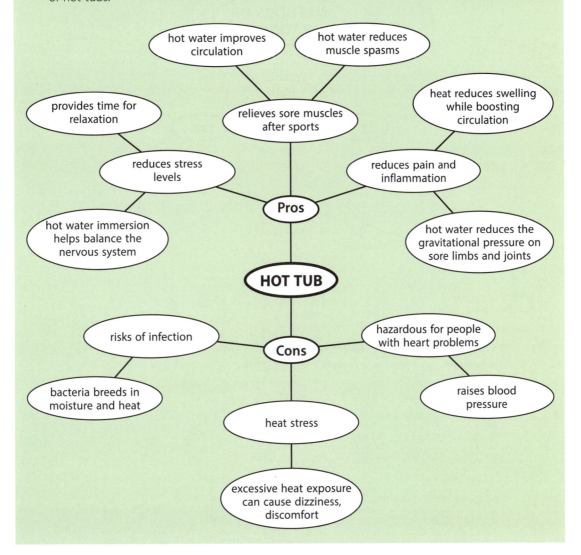

Unit 2 Hygiene 45

Exercise 2

Complete this cluster diagram on methods of bathing. Then study your diagram and decide what kind of essay you could develop.

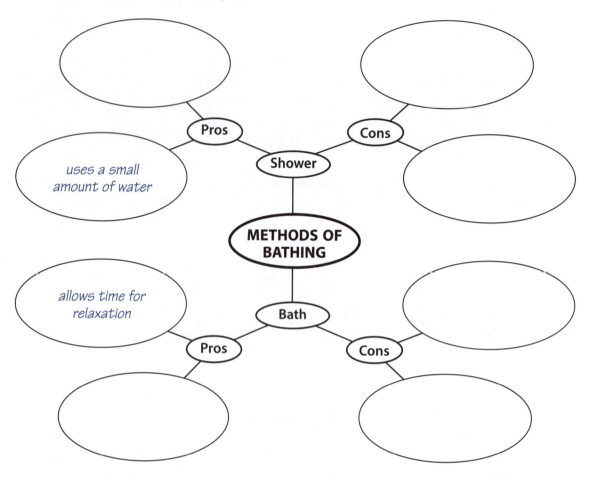

> **Freewriting**
>
> - With the *freewriting* technique, you write freely on a topic without stopping. You don't worry about correct grammar or whether what you think is important enough to write down. After you freewrite, you can decide which of your ideas could be useful.
>
> - Here are some steps to follow when freewriting.
>   1. Give yourself a time limit.
>   2. Write the topic at the top of your paper.
>   3. Write as much as you can about the topic. Don't worry about grammar, spelling, organization, or relevance.
>   4. Write until your time is up.
>   5. Read your freewriting and underline the main idea(s).
>   6. Repeat the process, this time using a main idea as your freewriting topic.
>
> - The following is an example of the freewriting technique applied to the subject of a vegetarian diet. Notice that the writer has underlined two ideas that could be explored further. The writer can take one of these ideas and freewrite about it again.

A Vegetarian Diet

I am not a vegetarian, but two of my friends are. They always tell me how cruel it is to kill animals, and I tell them I need meat to get my protein. They tell me you can get protein from sources other than animal products. <u>Animal products contain fat, which can be bad for health</u>, <u>whereas plants are high in fiber and good for health</u>. Even if it were good for me, I just think vegetarian food is boring. But they proved me wrong when I went out to eat with them. <u>The vegetarian dishes were very tasty</u>, <u>and there were so many varieties</u>. There are so many cookbooks now for vegetarians I noticed.

Exercise 3

Write freely without stopping for 10 minutes on the topic of good hygiene practices. Then underline ideas that you can explore further. The first sentence is done for you.

Good hygiene practices are essential for our health and social happiness.

Definitions

Sometimes a definition appears in an essay to clarify a word. The definition may be expressed in a sentence or a paragraph, or it may even be the entire essay. The reason for this is that there are two kinds of definitions: *literal definitions* and *extended definitions*.

Literal Definitions

- A *literal definition* gives the *literal* or dictionary meaning and is usually expressed in one sentence.

  EXAMPLE: Cleanliness is the state of being free from dirt.

- Many times, a form of the word or the word itself is used as part of the dictionary definition. This approach does not make the meaning clear. For example, avoid defining *cleanliness* as "the state of being clean." Your definition will be clearer if you say, "Cleanliness is the state of being free from dirt."

Extended Definitions

- When you want to give a personal interpretation of a word, you use an *extended definition*. The extended definition may differ from the literal meaning because the word is defined in a particular or personal way. The meaning of an abstract word or concept such as *cleanliness* is often given in an extended definition, because such a word can be interpreted in different ways.

  EXAMPLE:
  In America, clean means not only free of dirt but free of odor as well. When one bathes in Japan, it is about much more than cleanliness, though cleanliness is important. It is about family and community, the washing of each other's backs before bathing; about time to

be alone and contemplative—time to watch the moon rise above the garden. The idea of taking time and care with one's bath in Japan is as important as taking time and care with cooking and serving dinner.

- The extended definition involves various kinds of supporting ideas. Reading 1 tells how the word *cleanliness* was defined by the Romans and the Greeks and in the Middle Ages. We are then given examples of similarities and differences in ideas of cleanliness among different cultures today. In Reading 2, cleanliness is seen through the Japanese style of bathing. We are given the steps in the process of Japanese bathing, and we are told of the importance of cleanliness to the Japanese.

Etymology

- Sometimes the original meaning of a word is quite different from its present meaning, and you may want to show this. *The Oxford English Dictionary* and many other unabridged dictionaries give *etymologies*, the detailed histories of the origin and development of words.

Exercise 4

Determine if the following definitions are Accurate (*A*) or Inaccurate (*IA*). Rewrite the definitions that are inaccurate.

_____ 1. Thermostats are devices that regulate heaters and cooling machines, turning them on and off so that they maintain the required temperature.

_____ 2. Wind means destruction from devastating storms or benefits from harnessing energy with windmills.

_____ 3. Powered flight is the realization of man's fondest dream over thousands of years.

_____ 4. A keynote address is an opening address that outlines the issues to be considered.

_____ 5. A mammal is a vertebrate animal with self-regulating body temperature and the capability for milk production by the female.

_____ 6. Mountain sickness is a sickness people get when they are in the mountains.

_____ 7. Separation anxiety is a negative emotional state that occurs in small children when they are parted from their parents.

_____ 8. Good sense may be defined as something everyone should hope to have.

Exercise 5

Work with a partner, in a group, or alone. Look up the following words in a dictionary and write down their literal meanings. Then write three or four ways that the definitions might be extended to include personal, social, or cultural meanings. The first one is done for you.

1. touch

   Literal Meaning: *to bring a bodily part in contact with something*

   Extended Meaning: *Touch can take different forms and have different meanings. It can express politeness, friendship, or intimacy, for example.*

2. space

   Literal Meaning: _____

   Extended Meaning: _____

3. **time**

   Literal Meaning: _____

   Extended Meaning: _____

4. **smell**

   Literal Meaning: _____

   Extended Meaning: _____

5. **aggressiveness**

   Literal Meaning: _____

   Extended Meaning: _____

Exercise 6

The following terms have been defined using a form of the term itself. Rewrite each definition without repeating the term being defined. Make sure the meaning of the word is clear.

1. **fanaticism:** fanatic outlook or behavior
2. **loyalty:** the quality or state of being loyal
3. **happiness:** the state of being happy
4. **creativity:** the quality of being creative
5. **independence:** the quality or state of being independent

Exercise 7

Use an unabridged, big dictionary such as *Webster's New Collegiate Dictionary* or *The Oxford English Dictionary* to find the etymology of the words below. The first one is done for you.

1. **hygiene:**

   According to The Oxford English Dictionary hygiene comes from the Greek meaning the "art of health."

2. **clean:**

   _____

3. **relax:**

   _____

4. **health:**

   _____

5. **shampoo:**

   _____

The Definition Essay

A *definition essay* is a way for you to define and describe a term or a concept. The following are some points to help you organize a definition essay.

- In the **introduction** to a definition essay, state the term you are going to define. Then either define it yourself or use a dictionary definition, naming the dictionary and quoting from it. In your thesis statement, restate the term you are going to define and tell how you are going to define it, giving the three or four aspects from which you will illustrate your definition.

- Each **body paragraph** in your essay should illustrate an aspect of the definition that you stated in your thesis. Support each aspect with clear examples.

- The **conclusion** should summarize your personal definition and give a final comment on the term.

Writing Practice

Write an Essay

Choose one of the following topics to write a definition essay.

1. Honesty
2. Friendship
3. Respect

Pre-Write

A Use brainstorming or clustering to come up with ideas for your chosen topic.

B Now freewrite on your topic. Then underline any main ideas in your freewrite.

C Work on a thesis statement for your essay.

Organize Your Ideas

A Write your thesis statement.

B Write down at least three examples that illustrate the term that you have chosen to define in your essay.

C Make a detailed outline, showing what will be in the Introduction, Body, and Conclusion.

Write a Rough Draft

Using your detailed outline and any notes you made in Pre-Write, write a rough draft of your essay.

Revise Your Rough Draft

Check the thesis statement, unity, development, coherence and purpose of your rough draft.

Edit Your Essay

Work with a partner or your teacher to edit your essay. Check the spelling, punctuation, vocabulary, and grammar.

Write Your Final Copy

After you edit your essay, you can write your final copy.

Translation

A Translate the following passage into English.

中医在中国有超过2500年的历史，具有多种形式，包括草药医学、针灸（acupuncture）、按摩、食疗等。今天，中医在中国得到广泛运用，对我们的日常生活产生了巨大的影响。越来越多的中国人采用中医的各种疗法来调理自己的身体。在欧洲和北美，中医治疗开始越来越普遍，已经成为一种流行趋势。中医几乎不侧重于解剖结构（anatomical structure）而主要关注功能实体（entities）的鉴定（其调节消化、呼吸、老化等）。中医认为健康是这些实体与外部世界和谐的相互作用，而疾病则是这种相互作用的不调和。

B Translate the following passage into Chinese.

Hygiene pertains to the practices that prevent or minimize disease and the spreading of disease in homes and in everyday life settings such as social settings, public transport, the work place, public places, etc. Hygiene at home and in everyday life settings plays an important part in maintaining a healthy society. It includes procedures used in a variety of situations such as hand hygiene, respiratory hygiene, food and water hygiene, general home hygiene, care of domestic animals, and domestic healthcare. Preventing the spread of infectious diseases relies on breaking the chain of infection transmission. The simple principle is that, if the chain of infection is broken, infection cannot spread.

Weaving It Together

Unit Project

Choose one of the following topics and give a presentation on a definition of the topic to your classmates.

1. Honesty
2. Friendship
3. Respect

Searching the Internet

A Search the Internet for information about the ritual of space cleansing (or space clearing). Find answers to these questions:

1. What cultures practice this ritual?
2. When do they practice it?
3. Why do they practice it?
4. What are some of the things done in these rituals?
5. Who participates in these rituals?

B Search the Internet for extended definitions on two of the following terms. Share the information with your classmates.

| beauty | education | freedom | love | patriotism | prejudice |
| democracy | fanaticism | intelligence | nature | peace | trust |

C You may use your research later to write a definition essay.

What Do You Think Now?

Refer to the very beginning of this unit. Do you know the answers now? Complete the sentence, or circle the best answer.

1. The ancient _____ started public baths.
2. The average American today showers or bathes _____ times a week.
3. The Japanese (like/don't like) to have quick showers.
4. The Japanese (share/don't share) the same bathwater with other family members.

Broadening Your Horizon

A

Scientists Put Traditional Chinese Cures to the Test

As patients in the United States increasingly turn to acupuncture, herbal remedies, and other treatments of so-called alternative medicine, researchers are taking a much closer look to find out which techniques work, which are harmful, and which could lead to new medical insights.

B

Nutrition and Personal Hygiene

A balanced diet and good personal hygiene is essential to keeping healthy. The energy from your food influences your weight and sporting performance.

C

Poor Water and Hygiene "Kills Mothers and Newborns"

Many mothers and newborns are dying because of a lack of sanitation, safe water and hygiene while giving birth, leading health experts have warned.

UNIT
3

Humanitarians

Somali children being vaccinated by volunteer doctors on the Somali-Ethiopian border in August 2011

WHAT DO YOU THINK?

Answer these questions with your best guess. Circle *Yes* or *No*.

1. Do refugee camps provide shelter for people escaping from conflicts?   Yes   No
2. Can a group of children survive a journey alone across hundreds of miles?   Yes   No
3. Can a map help save people during a disaster?   Yes   No
4. Do international organizations provide the only aid in a crisis?   Yes   No

Reading ▪ 1

Pre-Reading

Preparing for the Reading Topic

A Discuss these questions with your classmates.

1. What are some qualities of born leaders?

2. Why does war create refugees? What are some places in the world that have refugee camps?

3. As refugees move from their homes to other places, what are some of the dangers they face along the way?

B With a partner, look at the following words or phrases. Use these words to create a description of someone's experience as if it were a true story.

burn	hide
chased by the enemy	safety
desert	starve
eat grass	thirsty
get sick	wild animals

Key Vocabulary

As you read "John Bul Dau and the 'Lost Boys of Sudan'", pay attention to the following words and see if you can work out their meanings from the contexts.

resilient	challenges
persevering	constantly
chaos	adjusted
survive	documentary
compassion	circumstances

John Bul Dau lays out bones made of paper and plaster in Washington, D.C., U.S.A., at an event drawing attention to genocide around the world.

John Bul Dau and the "Lost Boys of Sudan"

1   In Northeastern Africa from 1983 to 2005, when Sudan was one country, the Second Sudanese Civil War was fought between the north and south. During that time, about two million people died from war, hunger, and disease. Five million people were displaced, including the 27,000 "Lost Boys of Sudan" who were driven from their villages by the war. Among these boys was a **resilient**, **persevering**, and courageous born leader named John Bul Dau[1].

2   Dau's challenges began in 1987, when he was 13 years old. His village in the south was attacked by government troops from the north. As bullets from guns shrieked and his village burned, Dau made an escape. In the **chaos**, he became separated from his family and had to **survive** on his own. After a while, he joined thousands of other boys

---

1 John Bul Dau 约翰·布尔·道，苏丹迷途男孩的一员，著有《上帝不再眷顾我们》一书

Unit 3 Humanitarians   57

as they escaped on foot. We now know these boys as the "Lost Boys of Sudan". At that time, Dau didn't know that his journey would be over 1,000 miles (1,609 kilometers) long and last 14 years. He didn't know that he would survive his many trials, and show leadership, **compassion**, endurance, and the courage of a hero.

3   Many of the boys who escaped the fighting had been taking care of their cattle when the soldiers attacked their villages. They ran when they saw the soldiers coming and hid anywhere they could. At first, the boys were alone but eventually they came together as a group. As Dau and the other "Lost Boys" walked across Sudan, they faced many life-threatening **challenges**. Every day was a test of strength, courage, and endurance.

4   As the soldiers went after them, the boys encountered the added dangers of wild animals, hunger, thirst, and illness. Some boys were killed by lions. At night, the boys hid in trees to get away from the wild animals. They ate grass, tree leaves, and mud. Hunger and thirst were their constant companions. Like a herd of desperate antelope, they searched for water in a dry wilderness while keeping an eye out for their hunters. Their tongues were like sandpaper and their stomachs an empty, bottomless hole. They were barefoot and wore thin pieces of clothing that didn't protect them from the sun during the day and the cold desert at night. Many died, as death followed them like a hungry animal. And all the time, fear and loneliness hung over them like a dark cloud, and they thought **constantly** of their parents and longed to see their families again.

5   Yet Dau persevered courageously by putting one foot in front of the other along the endless journey ahead. He did not only think of himself. Caring and compassionate, he looked after the younger children, some only two or three years old. As one of the older boys, he led several groups on their journey over hundreds of miles. He was a young leader and a source of comfort for the suffering children.

John Bul Dau

6 Finally, the boys reached a refugee camp in Ethiopia[2]. It must have seemed like finding a lake in the desert. They found shelter there for almost four years. But war broke out there too, so the boys escaped back to Sudan. The Ethiopian soldiers pushed them to the border, where they had to cross the Gilo River[3]. The soldiers shot at them, so the boys jumped into the water. Many drowned because they couldn't swim. Others were eaten by crocodiles. And many were shot before they reached the other side.

7 Back in Sudan the boys went to a refugee camp, but there was no relief from their suffering. The government of the North heard that the boys had returned. Twice every day the military bombed the camp. The boys decided to move again. With the Northern Sudanese soldiers following them, many of the boys were killed or taken along the way. Somehow, Dau and the other survivors found the strength and courage to continue their escape to safety. Again, Dau showed his leadership, courage, and compassion as he cared for and led groups of boys on their journey.

8 Finally, they reached a refugee camp in Kenya[4], where Dau stayed for the next 10 years. Now 17, he attended school for the first time in his life. He started out with only sticks to write his numbers and letters on the ground. Nevertheless, Dau was a hard-working student. Determined not just to survive but somehow to succeed, he received the Kenya Certificate for Secondary Education.

9 Over the years, people around the world learned about the "Lost Boys". In the United States, several organizations started programs to resettle the refugees. In 2001, Dau became one of the 3,800 chosen to begin new lives in the U.S. He joined 140 who were brought to Syracuse[5], New York. Like so many others, Dau experienced culture shock in his new country. He felt like a fish out of water in the modern city. Everything was so different from anything he had ever known or experienced before. On his first trip to a supermarket, he may as well have been on the moon. But as he had shown time and again, John Bul Dau was a resilient young man. Eventually, he **adjusted** to his new life, and with his usual courage, determination, and hard work, he made another journey—this time on the road to success. Working 60 hours a week at two and sometimes three jobs, he earned enough to bring his mother and sister from Sudan. He also received an associate's degree[6] and a bachelor's degree from Syracuse University.

10 Dau's success was far from the end of his story. The leadership, compassion, and caring he showed as a young man followed him into adulthood and led him to start three nonprofit organizations. In 2003, he helped start the Sudanese Lost Boys Foundation of Central New York to raise money for education and medical expenses of the other "Lost Boys" living in the United States. Then in 2005, Dau was one of the founders of the American Care for Sudan Foundation, which raises money to build and operate clinics in Southern Sudan. In 2006, Dau told his life story in a co-authored book, *God Grew Tired of Us*. He wrote his story so people would learn about the "Lost Boys" and the people of Southern Sudan. A **documentary** was made with the same name, and it won awards. Dau believes there is a reason why he survived—to help his people.

---

2 Ethiopia 埃塞俄比亚，全名埃塞俄比亚联邦民主共和国，非洲东北部国家
3 Gilo River 吉罗河，埃塞俄比亚西南部甘贝拉州的河流
4 Kenya 肯尼亚，非洲东部国家，赤道横贯中部，东非大裂谷纵贯南北
5 Syracuse 锡拉丘兹，美国纽约州城市
6 associate's degree 美国大学修满两年课程的肄业证书，准学士学位

11   Today, John Dau is the president of both the John Dau Foundation and the South Sudan Institute. In his efforts to bring peace, hope, and help to the people of South Sudan he has won many awards and raised millions of dollars. Dau has also become a well-known speaker. He tells people to always be hopeful and to never give up, even when things are at their worst. Dau doesn't only speak those words. He is a living example of courage, resilience, and perseverance under the most hopeless and unimaginable **circumstances**. "Keep trying," he tells people. "You can't give up."

Vocabulary

Vocabulary in Context

A What are the meanings of the **bold** words? Circle the letter of the best answer.

1. Among these boys was a **resilient** leader named John Bul Dau.
    a. able to recover from difficulty
    b. brave in dangerous situations
    c. able to make good decisions
    d. honorable in one's actions

2. Among these boys was a **persevering**, courageous leader named John Bul Dau.
    a. telling the truth under any circumstance
    b. holding to a course in spite of difficulties
    c. being courageous in perilous situations
    d. coming up with new ideas to deal with problems

3. During the **chaos**, Dau became separated from his family.
    a. situation of grave danger
    b. surprising circumstance
    c. unusual state of affairs
    d. state of disorder and confusion

4. He had to **survive** on his own.
    a. go on with a journey
    b. find shelter
    c. move away from a place
    d. continue to live

5. Dau would show leadership and **compassion**.
    a. sympathy for the misfortune of others
    b. ability to take care of others
    c. capability to lead others
    d. ability to solve the problems of others

6. The boys faced many life-threatening **challenges**.
    a. journeys to take
    b. conflicts to solve
    c. trials to overcome
    d. decisions to make

7. They thought **constantly** of their parents.
    a. once in a while
    b. intermittently
    c. all the time
    d. periodically

8. In time, Dau **adjusted** to his new life.
    a. stayed with familiar ways
    b. changed to suit conditions
    c. got tired of current circumstances
    d. followed all the rules

9. A **documentary** was made and it won awards.

   a. film or program about imaginary people and places

   b. film or program that presents people's opinions about things

   c. film or program that presents facts

   d. film or program that combines true events with made-up drama

10. Dau is a living example of courage under the most unimaginable **circumstances**.

    a. journeys
    b. programs
    c. places
    d. conditions

B Answer these questions with complete sentences.

1. What **challenges** have you overcome?

2. What is one **documentary** film you have seen or want to see?

3. What does a mountain climber need to **survive**?

4. What is something you do **constantly** that you wish you didn't do?

5. What is an example of a **compassionate** action?

C Now write your own sentences. Use the following words in the sentences: **circumstances**, **persevering**, **adjusted**, **chaos**, and **resilient**.

Vocabulary Building

A Match the words in the reading that go together to make common phrases. The first one is done for you.

_d_ 1. keep   a. an escape
___ 2. made   b. leader
___ 3. born   c. organizations
___ 4. refugee   d. an eye out
___ 5. nonprofit   e. expenses
___ 6. medical   f. camp

B Complete the sentences with the words you matched in Exercise A.

1. John Bul Dau, one of the "Lost Boys", was a _____.

2. When the soldiers attacked his village, John Bul Dau _____.

Unit 3 Humanitarians 61

3. John Bul Dau and the boys stayed in a _____ in Ethiopia for four years.
4. As the boys walked in the wilderness, they had to _____ for wild animals.
5. After John Bul Dau came to the United States, he started three _____ to help the "Lost Boys".
6. He also started a Sudanese Lost Boys Foundation to get money for _____ and education for the other "Lost Boys" in the United States.

Reading Comprehension

A Circle the letter of the best answer.

1. Paragraph 2 is mostly about _____.
   a. the attack on Dua's village
   b. Dau's 1,000-mile journey
   c. what character traits Dau would show over the years
   d. how Dau became a "Lost Boy"

2. Paragraph 6 is mainly concerned with _____.
   a. life in an Ethiopian refugee camp
   b. war breaking out in Ethiopia
   c. the actions of the Ethiopian soldiers
   d. the boys' perilous escape from Ethiopia

3. Why did the boys decide to move from the refugee camp in Sudan?
   a. Because some boys found better shelter outside the refugee camp in some way.
   b. Because Dau could relieve other boys from suffering outside the refugee camp with his leadership, courage, and compassion.
   c. Because the military shot at the boys twice every day.
   d. Because the soldiers dropped bombs on the boys frequently.

4. It can be inferred from the reading that _____.
   a. people shouldn't go to refugee camps
   b. refugee camps can't always guarantee people's safety
   c. there aren't enough refugee camps for displaced people
   d. refugee camps don't provide good services

5. From the reading it can be concluded that _____.
   a. if it weren't for Dau, no one would have survived the journey across Sudan
   b. the dangers Dau and the other boys encountered were nothing compared with the difficulties they faced later in life
   c. the character traits that helped Dau survive his escape contributed to his success in adulthood
   d. the qualities needed to survive a perilous journey aren't necessarily helpful in ordinary life

B Complete the summary below using the list of words in the box.

survive	encounter	compassion	documentary	circumstances
efforts	challenges	resettle	raised	displaced
persevered	shrinking	shrieking	adjusted	rose

During the Second Sudanese Civil war which was fought between the north and the south from 1983 to 2005, millions of people, including nearly 30,000 "Lost Boys of Sudan", were **1.** _____ . As one of the boys, John Bul Bau saw bullets from guns **2.** _____ and his village burning. Dau had no choice but to leave his family and **3.** _____ all by himself. The journey of escaping for Dau and the other "Lost Boys" was really very hard. Every day, they would meet many **4.** _____ that could easily endanger their lives. However, on the long and hard journey, Dau not only **5.** _____ bravely, but he also showed leadership, **6.** _____ , endurance and the courage of a hero. Finally, these boys reached a refugee camp in Kenya, where Dau stayed for ten years. Fortunately, at that time, people around the world began to give a hand to these "Lost Boys". For example, several organizations began to **7.** _____ the refugees in the United States. In 2001, when Dau had the opportunity to live in Syracuse, New York, he experienced culture shock like other foreigners, but he finally **8.** _____ to his new life. In his life, he has tried to bring peace, hope, and help to his people. He has won many awards and **9.** _____ millions of dollars. Today, the public's behavior has been modeled upon his courage, resilience, and persistence in **10.** _____ which were desperate and difficult to imagine.

Critical Thinking

Discuss these questions with your classmates.

1. Dau believes his life's purpose is to help his people. Do you think there are certain people who are destined to do great things? Why or why not? What do you think is your life's purpose?
2. What is life like in a refugee camp? What are people's greatest needs?
3. Besides war, what are some other reasons why people become refugees? What emotions do you think refugees have?
4. What are the difficulties faced by displaced people (1) while they are on the move, and (2) once they arrive in areas outside their homelands?
5. What is the meaning of "culture shock"? Have you ever experienced it? What are some of the things people need to overcome culture shock if they settle in China?

Reading 2

Pre-Reading

Preparing for the Reading Topic

A Discuss these questions with your classmates.

1. What is a natural disaster? Give an example.

2. What is a man-made disaster? Give an example.

3. What kind of help do world organizations provide during disasters?

B Look at the list of items people might need during or after a disaster. Decide if an item is needed for a Natural Disaster (*ND*), a Man-made Disaster (*MD*), or Both (*B*).

_____ 1. food

_____ 2. temporary shelter from the elements

_____ 3. water

_____ 4. clothing

_____ 5. gas masks

_____ 6. peace-making force

_____ 7. long-term refugee camp

_____ 8. safe passage to another area

_____ 9. earth-moving equipment

_____ 10. healthcare workers

Key Vocabulary

As you read "Patrick Meier, Crisis Mapper", pay attention to the following words and see if you can work out their meanings from the contexts.

expose	crucial
rescue	resources
victims	witness
pioneers	option
accessible	integrates

Patrick Meier, who is currently the Director of Social Innovation at the Qatar Computing Research Institute, directs research on cutting-edge humanitarian technology solutions.

Patrick Meier, Crisis Mapper

1 **W**hat can speed humanitarian response to tsunami-ravaged coasts? **Expose** human rights atrocities? Launch helicopters to **rescue** earthquake **victims**? Outwit corrupt regimes?

2 A map.

3 But not just any map. Patrick Meier[1] **pioneers** the lifesaving new field of crisis mapping and makes it available, **accessible**, and free to humanitarian organizations and volunteers across the globe. As director of crisis mapping at the nonprofit technology company Ushahidi and co-founder of the Standby Volunteer Task Force, he

---

1 Patrick Meier 帕特里克·迈耶,国际公认的在人道主义救援技术和创新领域的专家和顾问

is helping to revolutionize the power and effectiveness of relief efforts worldwide.

4   Imagine the chaotic scene on the ground as any natural disaster or human rights crisis unfolds. Then imagine an online map lit up with **crucial** information pouring in, real time, reflecting exactly what is happening, what is most urgently needed, and precisely where.

5   Welcome to the 24/7 world of crisis mapping, where texts, tweets, emails, and mobile phone photos and videos meet the world's most highly respected, official players in humanitarian response. Meier is bringing the two worlds together for the first time, connecting an explosion of social media and satellite imagery with the United Nations, U.S. Marines[2] and Coast Guard[3], the World Health Organization[4], Amnesty International[5], and other groups that can mobilize help when the worst crises hit.

6   "Situational awareness is key to allocating **resources** and coordinating logistics," says Meier. "These dynamic ever-changing maps are like having your own helicopter. They provide a bird's-eye view as events unfold across time and space. Gaining information like this straight from crisis zones is a game changer[6]; these technologies didn't exist just a few years ago."

7   Meier's nonprofit company, Ushahidi, provides free, open-source[7] platforms that allow anyone in the world to gather information and use it to create live, crowd-sourced[8], multimedia maps. Ushahidi, which means "**witness**" in Swahili, began during Kenya's post-election violence in 2008.

8   "It was a simple Google map of Kenya with a form people could fill out to describe what they saw during the violence," he explains. "An SMS[9] **option** was also provided so people could send text messages." Since then, the technology has been refined and used in more than 140 countries with software available in 20 languages.

9   When crises occur, the Standby Volunteer Task Force gathers messages, photos, video, and high-resolution satellite imagery and **integrates** them on a live Ushahidi map. More than 800 volunteers from 80 different countries make up the decentralized network that works closely with local and international responders. The trained, tech-savvy mappers mobilize at a moment's notice. Since they occupy every time zone, work can continue around the clock. "Anyone can join and use a skill set they already have or learn a new one," says Meier. "These people are passionate about helping and making a difference."

---

2 U.S. Marines 美国海军陆战队
3 Coast Guard 海岸警卫队，即水上警察，是美国的一支军事化综合执法队伍
4 World Health Organization 世界卫生组织，联合国下属的一个专门机构，总部设置在瑞士日内瓦
5 Amnesty International 国际特赦组织
6 game changer 改变局面的新事物
7 open-source 开放源码的
8 crowd-sourced 众包的
9 SMS 短信服务

Vocabulary

A What are the meanings of the **bold** words? Circle the letter of the best answer.

1. It can **expose** human rights atrocities.
   a. hide away
   b. fight against
   c. make known
   d. examine closely

2. It can launch helicopters to **rescue** earthquake victims.
   a. treat for serious injuries
   b. provide needed supplies for
   c. make the situation better for
   d. save from harm or danger

3. It can launch helicopters to rescue earthquake **victims**.
   a. people who suffer harm because of something or someone else's actions
   b. people who are left to survive on their own
   c. people who are hurt because of their own actions or decisions
   d. people who are about to be harmed in some way

4. Patrick Meier **pioneers** the lifesaving new field of crisis mapping.
   a. does something first before everyone else
   b. makes something known to everyone else
   c. does something no one else could ever do
   d. creates something odd or unusual

5. Patrick Meier makes crisis mapping **accessible** and free.
   a. available in small quantities
   b. difficult to achieve
   c. open to possibility
   d. easy to obtain

6. Imagine an online map lit up with **crucial** information.
   a. in the largest quantity
   b. of the greatest importance
   c. of the most timely nature
   d. of the most truthful or realistic

7. "Situational awareness is key to allocating **resources** and coordinating logistics."
   a. changes that can be made at the last moment
   b. equipment that can be moved quickly
   c. people and supplies that can be used when needed
   d. information that can be sent to everyone

8. Ushahidi, which means "**witness**", began in 2008.
   a. a person who is an important part of an event
   b. a person who is present and sees something happen
   c. a person who likes to be in dangerous situations
   d. a person who makes good things happen

9. An SMS **option** was also provided.
   a. something required
   b. something new
   c. something provided all the time
   d. something offered as a choice

10. The Standby Volunteer Task Force **integrates** them on a live Ushahidi map.

   a. separates into many different parts
   b. makes stronger or more useful
   c. makes great use of
   d. brings together to form a whole

B Answer these questions with complete sentences.

1. What **option** would you like to have added to a new car?

2. What **resources** do you need for a camping trip?

3. What **rescue** might a firefighter make?

4. What is **crucial** to the success of a business?

5. Why do the police interview **witnesses** to a crime?

C Now write your own sentences. Use the following words in the sentences: *integrates*, *expose*, *accessible*, *victims*, and *pioneers*.

Reading Comprehension

A Circle the letter of the best answer.

1. Which of the following statements is a main idea of the reading?

   a. When crises happen, Standby Volunteer Task Force gathers messages, photos, and video from around the world.
   b. Information is shared with the United Nations and other organizations and groups.
   c. Patrick Meier has pioneered the lifesaving new field of crisis mapping.
   d. Trained mappers mobilize at a moment's notice.

2. Crisis mapping is available to _____ when crises hit.

   a. governments that aren't corrupt
   b. greatly admired humanitarian officials
   c. volunteers and institutions in humanitarian response
   d. trained, tech-savvy mappers

3. What does Ushahidi mean in Swahili language?

   a. Crowd-sourced multimedia map.
   b. Witness.
   c. Post-election violence.
   d. Open-source platform.

4. Which of the following statements is a fact mentioned in the reading?

   a. Relief efforts are more effective today thanks to the information provided by crisis mapping.

   b. Crisis mapping has improved greatly since it first started and is likely to get even better.

   c. Crisis mapping provides an opportunity for people to work together during a disaster.

   d. Patrick Meier is working to make radical changes to international relief efforts.

5. Which of the following statements can be inferred from the reading?

   a. At first, there was a simple Google map and a form on which people could describe what they saw during the violence.

   b. Software is now available in 20 languages, and there is an option for text messaging.

   c. Even people without specialized skills now have a place in the Standby Volunteer Task Force.

   d. Today's mappers are trained and tech-savvy.

B Find information in the reading to answer these questions. Note the number of the paragraph where you find the answer. Discuss your answers with a partner.

1. What can you imagine when a natural disaster or human rights crisis unfolds?

   _____

   _____

   Paragraph: _____

2. What kind of information do crisis maps contain?

   _____

   _____

   Paragraph: _____

3. Who make up the Standby Volunteer Task Force network?

   _____

   _____

   Paragraph: _____

Critical Thinking

Discuss these questions with your classmates.

1. Would you like to join the Standby Volunteer Task Force? Why or why not?

2. How might the crisis maps make a difference during a disaster? What are some other things people can do besides turning to the crisis maps when a disaster occurs in China?

3. People don't only need food and shelter after disasters. Many also need counseling. What emotional and psychological effects do disasters have on people?

4. What are the advantages of advanced technology in disasters? What can technology not do?

5. What are some of the problems that organizations face when they respond to disasters? How do corrupt governments prevent organizations from providing the help that victims need?

Writing

Writing Skills

Paraphrasing

When you *paraphrase*, you put information from another author into different words. In other words, you rephrase it without changing the meaning of the original. When you paraphrase, it is important to use your own words. A paraphrase should usually be the same length as the original passage so that it includes all the information.

- Although you are using your own words when you paraphrase, you are expressing another author's ideas. Therefore, you must be sure to give the author credit for them; otherwise, you will be plagiarizing. Begin your paraphrase with a reference to the author and/or title of the work or the source of the article. Use phrases such as:

    According to [author's name],...
    Based on [author's name]**'s article in** [source],...
    In [his/her] **book** [title], [author's name] **indicates that**...

- The following is an example of paraphrasing a paragraph titled "Ancient Medicine".

    Original Paragraph

    Medicinal practices in the ancient world were as related to religion and philosophy as they were to science. The Egyptians were proficient surgeons who employed an array of medications and surgical practices. Their extensive expertise involving the human anatomy was derived mainly from their practice of embalming. The ideology behind this was that the deceased person's spirit, or Ka, would perish if the body decomposed. To furnish an eternal abode for the spirit, the body was meticulously preserved. In another part of the ancient world, Chinese medicine was also linked to ideology, in particular the belief that people are closely linked to a universe dominated by two opposing types of forces known as *yin* and *yang*, the negative and the positive. Physicians were part philosophers who believed that the harmony of the universe and the health of people depended on keeping a balance between the two forces. (*Discovery*, Everett, Reid, and Fara)

    Paraphrase

    In their book *Discovery*, Everett, Reid, and Fara indicate that the practice of healing in the ancient world had as much to do with religion and philosophy as it did with science. Extremely skillful surgeons, the Egyptians used a variety of drugs and surgical techniques. Their broad knowledge of the human anatomy was primarily due to their preservation of the dead. Their belief was that the dead person's spirit, or Ka, would die if the body rotted away. To provide a lasting home for the spirit, the body was mummified as carefully as possible. In the ancient Far East, Chinese medicine also involved philosophical beliefs, especially the idea that people are part of a universe controlled by two conflicting forces known as *yin* and *yang*, the negative and the positive. Physicians endorsed the philosophical belief that the harmony of the universe and the health of people depended on keeping a balance between the two forces.

- Notice how the author of the paraphrase has substituted different words and phrases from the original.

Original	Paraphrase
medicinal practices	the practice of healing
were as related to	had as much to do with
proficient	extremely skillful
employed	used
array of medications	variety of drugs
practices	techniques
extensive expertise involving	broad knowledge of
was derived mainly from	was primarily due to
practice of embalming	preservation of the dead
the ideology behind this	their belief
deceased	dead
perish	die
decomposed	rotted away
to furnish an eternal abode	to provide a lasting home
meticulously preserved	mummified as carefully as possible
another part of the ancient world	the ancient Far East
was also linked to ideology	also involved philosophical beliefs
in particular the belief	especially the idea
closely linked to	part of
dominated	controlled
opposing	conflicting
were part philosophers who believed	endorsed the philosophical belief

- Some words in the original text cannot be changed because there are no synonyms for them, such as the names of people, countries, religions, and scientific terms. In "Ancient Medicine", for example, there are no synonyms for *Egyptians*, *science*, *Ka*, *Chinese*, *yin*, and *yang*. Not every word has to be changed in a paraphrase; a few of the original words may be kept to maintain the accuracy of a piece. In "Ancient Medicine", for example, important words like *ancient*, *religion*, *science*, *philosophy*, *anatomy*, *spirit*, *negative*, *positive*, *harmony*, and *universe* have not been changed.

> - Here are some useful steps to follow when paraphrasing.
>   1. Read the section of the book or article over several times until you fully understand it.
>   2. Underline any words you do not understand. Look them up in a dictionary or use a thesaurus to find a good synonym.
>   3. Begin your paraphrase with a reference to the author and/or title of the book or article.
>   4. Rewrite each sentence, simplifying the structure and using synonyms. Rewrite each sentence one after the other.
>   5. Review your paraphrase. Make sure it sounds natural and like your own writing. Check to see that you have included all the information in the original, and that you have not changed the meaning in any way.

Exercise 1

Working with a partner, in a group, or on your own, paraphrase the following selections. Use a dictionary or thesaurus to find synonyms. Follow the steps above.

1. Although many women throughout history have been involved in the development of science, their work has gained little recognition. For a number of reasons their achievements have been ignored and their names left out of books. (Everett, Reid, and Fara, *Discovery*, p. 92)

2. Observe a group of listeners the next time a good storyteller tells an obscene joke. Skilled joke tellers elaborate on details. They allow the tension to build gradually as they set up the punch line. Listeners smile or blush slightly as the joke progresses. According to Freud, this long building creates greater tension and thus a louder and longer laugh when the punch line finally allows a tension release. (Burger, *Personality*, p. 99)

3. Three decades of research has demonstrated that people exposed to aggressive models sometimes imitate the aggressive behavior. This finding holds true for children as well as adults. But clearly, simple exposure to an aggressive model is not enough to turn us into violent people. Anyone who has watched television or attended a few movies recently undoubtedly has seen some murders, beatings, shootings, and the like. Yet rarely do we leave the theatre in search of victims. (Burger, *Personality*, p. 445)

Exercise 2

Paraphrase Paragraph 3 from Reading 1.

_____
_____
_____
_____
_____

Simile and Metaphor in a Description Essay

A good descriptive essay often contains *figures of speech*, as well as the two elements mentioned in Unit 4, Book 2: *a dominant impression* and *appropriate supporting details*. In a descriptive essay, the writer uses figures of speech to make their descriptions more vivid. Figures of speech are colorful words and expressions, which may make some kind of comparison. We will look at two figures of speech: *the simile* and *the metaphor*.

- **Simile.** Of the many types of figures of speech, the simile provides the most direct comparison. In a simile, one thing is compared with another to show similarity, typically by using the word **like** or **as**.

    EXAMPLES: Their tongues were **like** sandpaper.

    These dynamic ever changing maps are **like** having your own helicopter.

- **Metaphor.** A metaphor expresses a comparison more indirectly, without using *like* or *as*. A word or phrase is used to suggest the strong likeness between the people or things being compared.

    EXAMPLE: Hunger and thirst were their constant companions.

    They provide a bird's-eye view as events unfold across time and space.

(The first metaphor compares hunger and thirst to constant companions. Companions are with us all the time and never leave our side. In the same way, the feelings of hunger and thirst never left the boys. The second metaphor compares the view a bird has from the sky with what the map provides. A bird can see everything below it for a great distance. In the same way, the map also shows everything that is going on around the world.)

Exercise 3

Complete the similes in the following sentences.

1. The volunteers for the Big Brothers Big Sisters program are as devoted as _____.
2. Sometimes Peace Corps volunteers have to be as tough as _____.
3. The Red Cross worker was as brave as _____.
4. A UNICEF worker can bring a smile to a child that is as bright as _____.
5. The Nature Conservancy believes plants and animals are as important as _____.
6. First-time volunteers are as enthusiastic as _____.
7. The medical team is as efficient as _____.
8. Their work is as desperately needed as _____.

Exercise 4

Work with a partner or a group. Explain the comparisons being made in the following metaphors.

1. Rescuing the survivors was a Herculean effort.
2. The arrival of the rescue team was a ray of sunshine.
3. After the war began, night descended on the country.
4. The volunteers lift the loads from the backs of the villagers.
5. Through their testimony, they hold a torch to the suffering of people everywhere.
6. Their knock on the door has saved the lives of many who had lost hope.

Writing Practice

Write an Essay

Choose one of the following topics to write a descriptive essay.

1. An organization, a society, or a club that you are familiar with
2. A tribe or group of people that you are familiar with
3. A person you know

Pre-Write

A Choose one or more of the pre-writing techniques described in Unit 2 to help you find ideas for your chosen topic.

B Determine the one dominant impression you want to make in your descriptive essay, then think of descriptive adjectives, supporting details and similes/metaphors to create that impression.

C Find an article that contains information on your topic. Find a short excerpt from the article that you would like to Include in your essay and paraphrase it.

D Work on a thesis statement for your essay.

Organize Your Ideas

A Write your thesis statement.

B Select two or three of the best adjectives from your Pre-Write exercise to describe your dominant impression.

C Find relevant descriptive details and effective similes or metaphors to support your dominant impression.

D Make a detailed outline, showing what will be in the Introduction, Body, and Conclusion.

Write a Rough Draft

Using your detailed outline and any notes you made in Pre-Write, write a rough draft of your essay.

Revise Your Rough Draft

Check the thesis statement, unity, development, coherence and purpose of your rough draft.

Edit Your Essay

Work with a partner or your teacher to edit your essay. Check the spelling, punctuation, vocabulary, and grammar.

Write Your Final Copy

After you edit your essay, you can write your final copy.

Translation

A Translate the following passage into English.

世界上最年轻的国家南苏丹正面临着人道主义危机,中国向南苏丹捐赠1700吨大米作为援助物资。根据联合国的数据,今年南苏丹粮食产量骤减,陷入严重的食物短缺危机。食物短缺甚至蔓延到南苏丹原来那些食物供应相对平稳的地区。中国对于南苏丹共和国每况愈下的人道主义状况很是担忧。捐赠大米是中国和南苏丹政府协商后的第一步举措。中国也将给予南苏丹政府医疗援助。此外,无论南苏丹面临怎样的挑战,中国将一如既往地给予支持。中国的这些举动无疑会拯救南苏丹人民的性命,还能缓解南苏丹政府的压力。

B Translate the following passage into Chinese.

For those of us on the ground in those early days, it was clear for the disaster-hardened veterans that Haiti was something different. Haiti provided us with something unprecedented, in a hyper-connected world where people had access to mobile smart devices. Here came a torrent of SMS texts—people crying for help, begging us for assistance, sharing data, offering support, looking for their loved ones. This was a situation that traditional aid agencies had never before encountered. We were unprepared for this, and they were shaping the aid effort. Outside Haiti also, things were looking different. Tens of thousands of so-called digital volunteers were searching the Internet, converting texts into tweets, and putting these onto open-source maps, layering them with other sorts of important information—people like Crisis Mappers—and putting these on the Web for everybody, the media, the aid organizations and the communities themselves to participate in and to use.

Weaving It Together

Unit Project

Choose one of the following topics and give a presentation on a description of the topic to your classmates.

1. An organization, a society, or a club that you are familiar with
2. A tribe or group of people that you are familiar with
3. A person you know

Searching the Internet

A Search the Internet for information about one of these international organizations: UNICEF, Oxfam, Africare, MercyCorps, Greenpeace, Friends of the Earth, or WaterAid. Find answers to these questions:

1. What does the organization do?
2. What areas of the world does the organization help?
3. Does the organization provide volunteer opportunities?
4. What can a volunteer do in this organization?

B Search the Internet for information on a humanitarian volunteer organization in China. Share the information with your classmates.

C You may use your research later to write a descriptive essay.

What Do You Think Now?

Refer to the very beginning of this unit. Do you know the answers now? Complete the sentence, or circle the best answer.

1. Refugee camps (provide/don't provide) shelter for people escaping from conflicts.
2. (Some/All) children can survive a journey alone across hundreds of miles.
3. A special kind of map called a(n) _____ can help save people during a disaster.
4. International organizations (provide/don't provide) the only aid in a crisis.

Broadening Your Horizon

A

The World Promises to Do a Better Job Aiding Refugees from Violence

It's one thing to make a pledge. But, will the participants in the first U.N. World Humanitarian Summit deliver?

B

Can Attacks on Aid Workers Be Stopped?

The attack on the trucks delivering humanitarian aid in Aleppo was potentially a war crime. But it's not likely anyone will go to jail for it. Is this the new normal?

C

The Outsiders

Has evolution programmed us to shun and turn our backs on refugees—even when they might die without our help?

UNIT 4
Psychology

WHAT DO YOU THINK?

Answer these questions with your best guess. Circle *Yes* or *No*.

1. Is there proof that the shape of your body and your character are connected? Yes   No
2. Are muscular people always dominant? Yes   No
3. Are introverts more responsive to caffeine than extraverts? Yes   No
4. Do extraverts like crowded social gatherings? Yes   No

Reading 1

Pre-Reading

Preparing for the Reading Topic

A Discuss these questions with your classmates.

1. How would you describe the personalities of the two men in the photo? What influenced your opinion?

2. Describe an incident in which you were wrong when you judged a person based on physical appearance.

3. Do people expect their leaders to look a certain way?

B Look at the photos of the two men again. Write *L* on the line if you think the adjectives below describe the man on the left. Write *R* on the line if you think the adjectives describe the man on the right.

_____ 1. athletic   _____ 7. reserved

_____ 2. bold   _____ 8. sensitive

_____ 3. anxious   _____ 9. studious

_____ 4. outgoing   _____ 10. aggressive

_____ 5. quiet   _____ 11. easygoing

_____ 6. intellectual   _____ 12. outgoing

Key Vocabulary

As you read "What Our Bodies Say About Us", pay attention to the following words and see if you can work out their meanings from the contexts.

lean	torso
hot-tempered	grace
enterprising	stooped
awkward	strides
meticulous	mean

What Our Bodies Say About Us

1 "Let me have men about me that are fat," says Julius Caesar[1] to Marcus Antonius[2] in Shakespeare's play *Julius Caesar*. In Julius Caesar's opinion, fat people were more trustworthy than thin ones—that is, those with a "**lean** and hungry look" who "are dangerous".

2 Shakespeare wasn't the first person to categorize personality according to body type. And if you've ever reacted to people based on the way they look, you know he wasn't the last. The relationship between physical characteristics and personality has been explored for thousands of years and used to predict and explain the actions of others. Although prehistoric man probably had his own ideas about the skinny guy in the cave next door, the ancient Greeks historically have been responsible for Western theories about body and character.

3 The Greeks believed the body was composed of four humors[3], or

---

1 Julius Caesar 尤利乌斯·凯撒（公元前100—前44），罗马共和国末期杰出的军事统帅和政治家
2 Marcus Antonius 马克·安东尼（公元前83—前30），古罗马政治家和军事家
3 humor （旧时生理学所说动物的）体液

Unit 4 Psychology   81

Figure 1.
Body Shapes

Endomorph Mesomorph Ectomorph

fluids: blood, black bile[4], yellow bile, and phlegm. The fluid someone had the most of determined his or her temperament or personality type—sanguine (hopeful), melancholic (sad), choleric (**hot-tempered**), or phlegmatic (dull or slow). Although this ancient theory eventually lost its popularity, it was replaced over the next few thousand years by all kinds of other ways to identify and catalog people by type. One of the most popular modern theories was proposed by William Sheldon[5] in the late 1940s and early 1950s. He suggested a relationship between body shape and temperament (see Figure 1). According to Sheldon's system, the *endomorph*[6]—with an oval-shaped body and large, heavy stomach—is slow, sociable, emotional, forgiving, and relaxed. The *mesomorph*[7]—with a triangular shape and a muscular, firm, upright body, is confident, energetic, dominant, **enterprising**, and at times hot-tempered. The *ectomorph*[8]—with a thin, fragile body—is tense, **awkward**, and **meticulous**.

4   A number of researchers since Sheldon have contributed their own ideas to the basic theory that body shape and personality are somehow connected. Going one step beyond basic shape is the idea of "body splits". This theory looks at the body in sections—top to bottom, front to back, **torso** and limbs—with the idea that each part of the body tells its own story. For example, the upper half of the body, consisting of the chest, head, and arms, is expressive and conveys our feelings to others through gestures and facial movements. The lower body, on the other hand, is associated with more deeply felt emotions—particularly those about family, children, and self-image.

---

4 bile 胆汁
5 William Sheldon 威廉·谢尔登，美国心理学家
6 endomorph 胖型体质者，内胚层体型者
7 mesomorph 运动型体质者
8 ectomorph 瘦型体质者，外胚层体型者

5   According to this theory, someone with a well-developed upper body will be active and outwardly confident. However, if this same person has noticeably thinner legs and narrow hips, he or she might have trouble expressing himself or herself to others, lack self-confidence, and find it difficult to think about deep emotions. A person with a small chest but large hips will have opposite traits, such as being shy in public, but emotional and loving towards friends and family. Look for many clues to personality: weight distribution (heaviness or thinness in different parts of the body), muscular development, **grace** and coordination, and general health. For example, does one half of the body seem healthier, or more tense, or more relaxed than the other? Look for tense shoulders or stiff legs and hips.

6   Backs and fronts are different, too. The front of the body is associated with our conscious self, the one we think about and show to others. The back, which is hidden from us most of the time, is associated with our unconscious self—that is, the feelings we hide from both ourselves and others. Many times, we don't want to think about or show emotions such as anger and fear, and we tend to store these feelings in the back. If you're feeling stress, your back is likely to be tense. People who find it hard to deal with problems without losing their temper are likely to have some kind of back trouble. Look around you at the stories backs tell. A **stooped** back is weighed down by burdens or troubles. A stiff and rigid back is hiding anger or stress. A straight and graceful spine is strong and flexible. Do you know what kind of back you have?

7   Finally, there is the split between the torso, or body, and the limbs, or arms and legs. You express yourself with your arms and hands, and even your legs in the way you move about. People who are outgoing often use their hands and arms to gesture when they talk. They also walk with long, confident **strides**. Shy people hold their hands and arms quietly close to them and walk with small steps. Energetic people often tap their feet and move around a lot because it's hard for them to sit still. They can sometimes be impatient and are not the best listeners.

8   There is no end to theories about body shape and personality, and there is no doubt that certain people with certain bodies often have very predictable characters. However, there are some researchers who believe that the many instances in which body and personality go together are due to stereotyping; that is, we expect a certain type of person to have certain traits, so we see those traits whether they are there or not. For example, muscular people are believed to be dominant and forceful, so we treat them as leaders. But sometimes they are actually shy and timid. Fat people are supposed to be happy and warmhearted, but in reality they can just as easily be depressed or **mean**. Sometimes people will even act the way they think others expect them to act. By doing that, people fill the role in which we picture them.

9   No matter how you look at it, bodies and personalities are related, whether by chance or by choice. However, there are always exceptions to the rule—and whenever that happens, there goes the theory. After all, we're only human; and that means we have a mind of our own—whether we're fat, skinny, or something in between.

Vocabulary

Vocabulary in Context

A What are the meanings of the **bold** words? Circle the letter of the best answer.

1. According to Shakespeare's *Julius Caesar*, people with a "**lean** and hungry look" are dangerous.
    a. wild
    b. thin
    c. weak
    d. angry

2. The Greeks believed a choleric person was **hot-tempered**.
    a. lively
    b. romantic
    c. easily angered
    d. enthusiastic

3. The person with a triangular shape is confident, dominant, and **enterprising**.
    a. possessing the courage to start new and difficult things
    b. ready to attack at any time
    c. possessing special skills in business
    d. fond of being in control

4. The person with a thin, fragile body is tense and **awkward**.
    a. not friendly to people
    b. not very active or worried
    c. lacking in ability to make decisions
    d. lacking in skill in moving his or her body

5. The thin, fragile *ectomorph* is also **meticulous**.
    a. concerned about details
    b. concerned about spending money
    c. unable to decide
    d. unable to relax

6. Each section of the body—top to bottom, front to back, **torso** and limbs— tells its own story.
    a. the head and shoulders
    b. the body without the head, legs, and arms
    c. the front of the head and body
    d. the body with the head, but without the legs and arms

7. Look for clues to personality such as weight distribution, muscular development, **grace** and coordination, and general health.
    a. beauty and harmony in movement
    b. beauty of physical features
    c. healthy color of physical features
    d. straight and flexible body

8. A **stooped** back is weighed down by troubles.
    a. hardened
    b. painful
    c. tense
    d. bent

9. People who are outgoing walk with long, confident **strides**.
    a. movements
    b. steps
    c. gestures
    d. manners

10. Fat people can just as easily be depressed or **mean**.
    a. unkind
    b. moody
    c. anxious
    d. gloomy

B Answer these questions with complete sentences.

1. Who is a person you think has **grace**?
   _____

2. When do you take long **strides**?
   _____

3. How would a **meticulous** person write an essay?
   _____

4. What can protect the head and the **torso** in a car accident?
   _____

5. What is a sport where the participants are usually **lean**?
   _____

C Now write your own sentences. Use the following words in the sentences: **hot-tempered**, **enterprising**, **mean**, **stooped**, and **awkward**.

_____
_____
_____
_____

Vocabulary Building

A Find the words below in the reading. Then notice the words that go with them in the reading. Write those words on the blank lines to make phrases. The first one is done for you.

1. active and _confident_
2. burdens and _____
3. anger and _____
4. dominant and _____
5. shy and _____
6. happy and _____

B Complete these sentences with the words you found in Exercise A.

1. A person who is _____ likes to talk a lot.
2. A(n) _____ person is afraid of everything.
3. A(n) _____ person is very generous.
4. People who have a lot of _____ may even be afraid to leave their homes.
5. If you have a lot of _____, you will get sick more often.
6. A person who uses strength to get his or her own way is _____.

Reading Comprehension

A Circle the letter of the best answer.

1. The main idea of Paragraph 3 is that _____.
   a. the Greek theory of personality lost its popularity over the years
   b. many personality theories had been developed by the 1940s and 1950s
   c. William Sheldon's theory relates body shape to personality
   d. large, heavy people are usually sociable and emotional

2. Paragraph 6 is mostly about _____.
   a. the difference between a person's front and back
   b. how stress and anger can cause back problems
   c. how we hide our feelings from ourselves and others
   d. what a person's back can reveal about him or her

3. Fat people are stereotyped as _____.
   a. happy and warmhearted
   b. dominant and forceful
   c. shy and timid
   d. depressed and mean

4. The reading implies that _____.
   a. ancient people didn't know enough to understand personality theories
   b. very few theories that categorize people by their appearance have been popular
   c. it's natural for people to look for relationships between physical characteristics and personality
   d. it takes a scientific mind to identify and categorize people according to body type

5. From the reading, it can be concluded that _____.
   a. our emotions and attitudes can affect our health and appearance
   b. a person with a pleasant personality is most likely to be pear-shaped
   c. the shape of the body as a whole tells the most about personality
   d. it's easy to hide our emotions from others

B Complete the summary below using the list of words in the box.

instances	focuses	mean	predictable	meticulous
awkward	grace	exceptions	aggressive	sanguine
sociable	timid	enterprising	hot-tempered	stereotyping

In the reading, the author 1. _____ on different theories about the relationship between physical characteristics and personality. According to the Greek theory, there are four body fluids, each with its own related personality type: blood, producing a 2. _____, or hopeful, temperament; black bile, producing a melancholic, or sad, temperament; yellow bile, producing a choleric, or 3. _____, temperament; and phlegm, producing a phlegmatic, or lazy or slow, temperament. According to Sheldon's system, people can be divided into three shapes: the *endomorph* is slow, **4.** _____, emotional, forgiving, and relaxed; the *mesomorph* is confident, energetic, dominant, **5.** _____, and at times hot-tempered; and the *ectomorph* is tense, awkward, and **6.** _____. In the theory of "body splits", four clues to personality are weight distribution, muscular development, **7.** _____ and coordination, and general health. These theories about body shape and personality claim that there is no doubt that certain people with certain bodies often have very **8.**_____ characters. However, some researchers believe that the many **9.** _____ in which body and personality go together are due to **10.** _____. Despite the different opinions, the author believes that bodies and personalities are related, whether by chance or by choice.

Critical Thinking

Discuss these questions with your classmates.

1. How can gestures and body movement be used to classify people?
2. What do you think of Sheldon's theory of relating body type to personality? Do you agree or disagree with him? Why or why not?
3. Since ancient times, people have tried to classify humans by personality type. Why do you think people have always been so fascinated with this subject?
4. What does categorizing people allow us to do? How can it be a benefit? How can it be harmful?
5. How do you develop your own theory of personality types based on your own experiences and observations?

Reading 2

Pre-Reading

Preparing for the Reading Topic

A Discuss these questions with your classmates.

1. Which would you prefer, a loud party with lots of people or a quiet dinner with a few friends? What do you think your answer says about your personality?

2. How do our daily habits reveal something about our personalities? What do your daily habits reveal about your personality?

3. Do you think people's personalities can be divided into various categories? What are some categories into which we place people?

B Psychologists often describe people as being extraverted (sociable) or introverted (quiet). Write *E* on the line if you think the phrases below describe an Extravert. Write *I* on the line if you think the phrases below describe an Introvert.

_____ 1. doesn't like to read

_____ 2. likes loud parties

_____ 3. has just a few close friends

_____ 4. doesn't like crowds

_____ 5. does not like to be alone

_____ 6. doesn't need to have people around

_____ 7. doesn't like noisy places

_____ 8. likes being alone and quiet

_____ 9. has many friends

_____ 10. likes to talk to people

Key Vocabulary

As you read "Why We Are What We Are", pay attention to the following words and see if you can work out their meanings from the contexts.

hierarchically	introspective
dimension	stimulation
impulsive	aversive
uninhibited	ample
retiring	subtle

Why We Are What We Are

The following reading is taken from Personality, *a college psychology text written by Jerry Burger[1] and published by Wadsworth[2], a division of Thomson Learning[3], Belmont[4], CA, 2000. In Chapter 9, "The Biological Approach", Hans Eysenck[5]'s theory of personality is described. Eysenck claims that differences in personality are based on biological differences.*

1   Eysenck's research strategy begins by dividing the elements of personality into various units that can be arranged **hierarchically**. The basic structure in this scheme is the *specific response level*, which consists of specific behaviors. For example, if we watch a man spend the afternoon talking and laughing with friends, we would be observing a specific response. If this man spends many afternoons each week having a good time with friends, we have evidence for the second level in Eysenck's model, a *habitual response*. But it is likely that this man doesn't limit himself to socializing just in the afternoon and just with these friends. Suppose this man also devotes a large part of his weekends and quite a few evenings to his social life. If you watch long enough, you might find that he lives for social gatherings, discussion groups, parties, and so on. You might conclude, in Eysenck's terms, that this person exhibits the *trait* of sociability. Finally, Eysenck argues that traits such as sociability are part of a still larger **dimension** of personality. That is, people who are sociable also tend to be **impulsive**, active, lively, and excitable. All these traits combine to form the *supertrait* Eysenck calls *extraversion*.

2   How many of these supertraits are there? Originally, Eysenck's factor analytic research yielded evidence for two basic dimensions that could subsume all other traits: *extraversion-introversion* and *neuroticism*. Because the dimensions are independent of one another, people who score on the extraversion end of the first dimension can score either high or low on the second dimension. Further, as shown in Figure 1, someone who scores high on extraversion and low on neuroticism possesses different traits than does a person who scores high on both extraversion and neuroticism.

3   Where do you suppose you fall in this model? If you are the prototypic extravert, then Eysenck describes you as "outgoing, impulsive, and **unin-hibited**, having many social contacts and frequently taking part in group activities. The typical extravert is sociable, likes parties, has many friends, needs to have people to talk to, and does not like reading or studying by himself." An introvert is "a quiet, **retiring** sort of person,

---

1 Jerry Burger 杰里·伯格，美国人格心理学家
2 Wadsworth 沃兹沃思出版社
3 Thomson Learning 汤姆森学习出版集团
4 Belmont 贝尔蒙特，美国加利福尼亚州西部城市
5 Hans Eysenck 汉斯·艾森克（1916–1997），英国心理学家

introspective, fond of books rather than people; he is reserved and distant except to intimate friends." Of course, most people fall somewhere between these two extremes, but each of us is perhaps a little more of one than the other.

4   Eysenck argues that extraverts and introverts differ not only in terms of behavior but also in their *physiological* makeup. Eysenck originally maintained that extraverts and introverts have different levels of *cerebral cortex arousal*[6] when in a nonstimulating, resting state. Although it may sound backward at first, he proposed that extraverts generally have a *lower* level of cortical arousal than do introverts. Extraverts seek out highly arousing social behavior *because* their cortical arousal is well below their desired level when doing nothing. In a sense, highly extraverted people are simply trying to avoid unpleasant boredom. Their problem is feeding their need for **stimulation**. Introverts have the opposite problem. They typically operate at an above-optimal cortical arousal[7] level. These people select solitude and nonstimulating environments in an effort to keep their already high arousal level from becoming too **aversive**. For these

---

6 cerebral cortex arousal 大脑皮层唤醒度
7 above-optimal cortical arousal 高于最优脑皮层唤醒度

reasons, extraverts enjoy a noisy party that introverts can't wait to leave.

5   Unfortunately, a great deal of research has failed to uncover the different levels of base-rate cortical arousal[8] proposed by Eysenck. For example, introverts and extraverts show no differences in brain-wave activity when at rest or when asleep (Stelmack[9], 1990). But this does not mean that Eysenck's original theorizing was entirely off base. Rather, there is **ample** evidence that introverts are more sensitive to stimulation than extraverts are (Stelmack, 1990). That is, introverts are more quickly and strongly aroused when exposed to loud music or the stimulation found in an active social encounter. Introverts are even more responsive than extraverts when exposed to chemical stimulants, such as caffeine or nicotine.

6   Consequently, many researchers now describe extraverts and introverts in terms of their different sensitivity to stimulation, rather than the different base rate of cortical activity Eysenck proposed. However, the effect is essentially the same. Because of

---

8 base-rate cortical arousal 基本脑皮质唤醒度
9 Stelmack 斯戴尔麦克（Robert M. Stelmack），加拿大心理学家

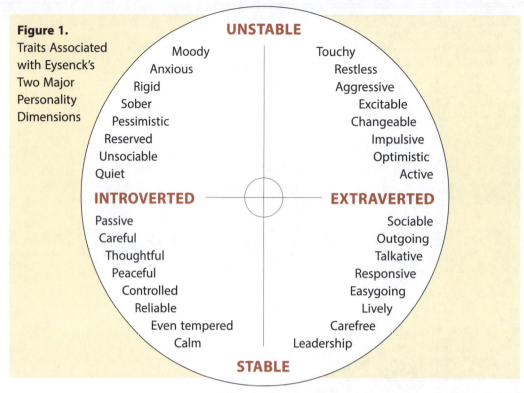

Figure 1. Traits Associated with Eysenck's Two Major Personality Dimensions

physiological differences, introverts are more quickly overwhelmed by the stimulation of a crowded social gathering, whereas extraverts are likely to find the same gathering rather pleasant. Extraverts are quickly bored by slow-moving movie plots and soft music because they are less likely to become aroused by these **subtle** sources of stimulation than introverts are.

Vocabulary

A What are the meanings of the **bold** words? Circle the letter of the best answer.

1. Eysenck divided the elements of personality into units that can be arranged **hierarchically**.

    a. evenly
    b. randomly
    c. from higher to lower
    d. in groups

2. Traits are part of a larger **dimension** of personality.

    a. subject
    b. aspect
    c. division
    d. range

3. People who are sociable also tend to be **impulsive**.

    a. kind
    b. arrogant
    c. hasty
    d. cautious

4. Eysenck describes extraverts as "outgoing, impulsive, and **uninhibited**."

    a. generous with money
    b. free and open
    c. unimaginative
    d. undependable

5. An introvert is "a quiet, **retiring** sort of person."
   a. possessing an excellent memory
   b. attending to duties willingly
   c. not fond of work
   d. tending to avoid the company of others

6. Eysenck thinks introverts are **introspective** and fond of books.
   a. thoughtful
   b. tolerant
   c. patient
   d. easygoing

7. Highly extraverted people try to feed their need for **stimulation**.
   a. excitement
   b. relaxation
   c. knowledge
   d. success

8. Introverts select nonstimulating environments in an effort to keep their already high arousal level from becoming too **aversive**.
   a. unimportant
   b. unpleasant
   c. unnecessary
   d. unsafe

9. There is **ample** evidence that introverts are more sensitive to stimulation than extraverts are.
   a. less than might be expected
   b. incomplete
   c. plenty of
   d. exactly enough

10. Extraverts are less likely to become aroused by **subtle** sources of stimulation than introverts are.
    a. hardly noticeable
    b. very unusual
    c. extremely displeasing
    d. constant

B Answer these questions with complete sentences.

1. What environment do you find **aversive**?

2. When cooking, what spice has a **subtle** flavor?

3. What is a job where there is **ample** opportunity to meet people?

4. What is something that an **introspective** person would like to do?

5. What **stimulation** is relaxing for you?

C Now write your own sentences. Use the following words in the sentences: ***dimension***, ***impulsive***, ***retiring***, ***uninhibited***, and ***hierarchically***.

Reading Comprehension

A Circle the letter of the best answer.

1. What is the main idea of Paragraph 1?

    a. Eysenck believes that we can infer a person's habitual responses by watching his or her specific responses.

    b. Eysenck argues that the trait of sociability exhibits the dimension of extraversion.

    c. Eysenck divided the elements of personality into various units based upon behavior.

    d. There are five units in Eysenck's research on personality, which can be arranged hierarchically.

2. Eysenck's original theory divided personality into _____.

    a. three basic dimensions

    b. several supertraits

    c. impulsive and outgoing behavior

    d. extraversion-introversion and neuroticism

3. Eysenck thought that, compared to introverts, extraverts had _____.

    a. a higher level of cortical arousal

    b. nearly the same level of cortical arousal

    c. a lower level of cortical arousal

    d. a different kind of cortical arousal

4. Which statement cannot be inferred from the reading?

    a. An introvert's discomfort might be mistaken for unfriendliness.

    b. An extravert isn't easily embarrassed.

    c. An introvert would like a museum better than a crowded movie theater.

    d. An extravert likes people more than he or she needs them.

5. From the reading, it can be concluded that _____.

    a. Eysenck didn't spend enough time studying people to come up with a good personality theory

    b. Eysenck's theory is not right since introverts and extraverts show no differences in brain-wave activity when at rest or when asleep

    c. physiological differences between introverts and extraverts are believed to exist by many researchers nowadays

    d. introverts are more intelligent than extraverts

B Find information in the reading to answer these questions. Note the number of the paragraph where you find the answer. Discuss your answers with a partner.

1. How did Eysenck describe the prototypic extravert and introvert in his model?

    _____

    _____

    Paragraph: _____

2. How did Eysenck explain the difference between extraverts and introverts in terms of their physiological makeup?

   _____

   _____

   Paragraph: _____

3. What might be the explanation of the difference between extraverts and introverts given by researchers nowadays?

   _____

   _____

   Paragraph: _____

Critical Thinking

Discuss these questions with your classmates.

1. To what extent is personality hereditary? What other factors do you think affect the development of someone's personality?

2. Do you think most people are happy with the personality they have? Do you think it's possible to change your personality? Why, or why not? If you could change your personality, what kind of person would you become?

3. What kind of partner would you like to work with, a partner whose personality type is like yours or opposite to yours? Explain.

4. Do you think Eysenck's theory makes sense? Why, or why not? What would you add to either support Eysenck's theory or to prove it wrong?

5. In what ways does personality affect a person's behavior, lifestyle, and choice of profession? Imagine a day in the life of an introvert and a day in the life of an extravert. What would those days be like? Explain.

Writing

Writing Skills

Writing a Summary

A *summary* is very similar to a paraphrase, only shorter. When you summarize, you put published information in your own words and include all the important information, without changing its meaning, just as you do when you paraphrase. However, when you summarize, you reduce the amount of information. The length of summaries varies. For example, the summary of a book may be several pages long, while the summary of an article may be one paragraph.

- In a summary, only the main ideas and key points are stated, and repetitions of the same idea are left out. Since you include only the main ideas in a summary, it is helpful to make a brief outline before you begin to summarize.

- The paragraph below is followed by an example of how it could be outlined and then summarized.

Original Paragraph

What kind of people are likely candidates for heart attacks and what kind are not? Typical Type A people are the most susceptible to heart problems, because they are strongly motivated to overcome obstacles and are driven to achieve and to meet goals. They are attracted to competition, enjoy power and recognition, and are easily aroused to anger and action. They dislike wasting time and do things in a vigorous and efficient manner. On the other hand, Type B people are relaxed and unhurried. They may work hard on occasion, but rarely in the driven, compulsive manner of Type A people. These people are less likely than Type A's to seek the stress of competition or to be aroused to anger or action. Naturally not all people classified as Type A or Type B fit these profiles exactly, and there are times when Type A people behave in a Type B manner and vice versa. But, as with other traits, researchers can identify the extent to which each of us behaves, on the average, and assign us a personality type on the basis of which some startling predictions can be made. (*Personality*, Burger)

Outline

A. Type A people
   1. at risk for heart attacks
   2. driven, competitive, quick-tempered, time-conscious, energetic, and efficient
B. Type B people
   1. calm and unhurried
   2. less competitive and slower to react
C. On the basis of average behavior, people can be categorized according to well-defined personality types.

Summary

According to Burger in his book *Personality*, people can be categorized into well-defined personality types on the basis of their average behavior. Type A people tend to be more at risk for heart attacks because they are driven, competitive, quick-tempered, time-conscious, energetic, and efficient. Type B people, on the other hand, are calm, unhurried, less competitive, and less reactive than their Type A counterparts.

You can see from the outline that the main idea (Item C) is stated in the last sentence of the passage. In your summary, however, you write the main idea first and then add one sentence for each of the two supporting ideas (Items A and B).

Exercise 1

Summarize the following passages in a few sentences. Then check your summary using the summary checklist below.

Summary Checklist
- [ ] Begin with a reference to the author and/or title of the book or article. Include the source of the article.
- [ ] Identify and write the main ideas and key points.
- [ ] Do not include details or repeat ideas.

1. Music video is a relatively new entry into the world of television, having become common only in the 1980s. Music video is difficult to categorize and to illustrate with one example, because it includes so many different types of expression. The definitive characteristic is in its name: There is music and there is video imagery. Some music videos dramatize the words of a song or even create brief visual dramas that are only vaguely related to the music. Some offer a message or statement. Some are relatively straightforward recordings of the performers at work. Obviously, defining the art of music video is not an easy task. (*Living with Art*, Rita Gilbert)

2. Beginning in the Middle East at least 10,000 years ago, some peoples began to purposely sow the seeds of their food plants. It was a practice that allowed them to produce adequate amounts of food in the areas near their settlements rather than pursuing game and living as nomads. At the same time, they gradually tamed and domesticated wild animals for their food, hides, and labor. An agricultural lifestyle led to the first towns and cities, the development of tools, baskets and pots, which led to the development of commerce and new crafts and skills. Agriculture played a significant role in developing the control over our existence that distinguishes humans from other species. (*Biology!* Postlethwait, Hopson, and Veres)

3. Charles Darwin, an English naturalist and explorer, began a five-year expedition in December 1831 on a ship called the *Beagle*. The expedition reached Bahia in Brazil in the spring of 1832. Darwin was amazed by the number and dazzling colors of the flowers and birds he saw. The *Beagle* then sailed south along the coast of Patagonia where the crew discovered the fossil remains of several extinct animals. In September 1835, the expedition reached the remote Galapagos Islands. There Darwin saw birds, animals, and plants that are found nowhere else on earth because they had developed in isolation from their relatives in America. They were to play an important part in Darwin's theories on how animals and humans evolved. (*Discovery*, Everett, Reid, and Fara)

Exercise 2

Write a summary of "Why We Are What We Are". Then check your summary using the summary checklist in Exercise 1.

_____
_____
_____
_____

The Principle of Classification

Classification means dividing people, objects, places, or ideas into various groups so that members of each group share similar characteristics. With this method, we give order to the many things in this world. Sociologists classify people into different classes; biologists classify plants or animals into species; and psychologists classify people's personalities into various types.

- To be clear, a classification should be based on a single principle. This means that you must choose one criterion on which to make your classification. In Reading 1 on body language, Sheldon classified people into three types—the endomorph, the mesomorph, and the ectomorph—based on the principle of body type. In Reading 2, Eysenck classified people into extraverts and introverts based on the principle of personality. In your classroom, you could classify the students according to their ethnicity: Han, Zhuang, Manchu, etc. You could also classify the same students according to their age: under 18, between 18 and 20, over 20. Another classification of the same students could be according to their work in class: hardworking students, average students, lazy students. Yet another classification could be made based on where they sit in class: in the front rows, in the middle, in the back rows.

Exercise 3

Identify one item in each of the following groups, and say how it is different from the others in that group. The first one is done for you.

1. **vehicles:** car, truck, van, jeep, motorcycle
   Motorcycle does not belong. All the others have four wheels.

2. **sports:** football, baseball, tennis, volleyball, swimming

3. **literature:** poetry, newspaper article, short story, drama, novel

4. **transportation:** by land, by air, by sea, by bus

5. **teachers:** bachelor's degree, master's degree, Ph.D., brilliance

6. **style of clothes:** formal, semiformal, casual, beachwear

7. **sports:** hiking, skiing, swimming, ice skating, tennis

8. **animals:** tortoise, crocodile, snake, lizard, monkey

9. **food:** protein, carbohydrates, fats, minerals, sugar

10. **drugs:** stimulants, depressants, hallucinogens, sedatives

Exercise 4

Look at the following subjects and categories. Identify the principle of classification being used. The first one is done for you.

1. **students:** intelligent, average, below average

    Principle of classification: _level of intelligence_

2. **teachers:** tough graders, fair graders, easy graders

    Principle of classification: _____

3. **people:** round faces, diamond-shaped faces, rectangular faces, square faces, triangular faces

    Principle of classification: _____

4. **people:** dark hair, blond hair, red hair

    Principle of classification: _____

5. **drivers:** very careful, careful, careless, reckless

    Principle of classification: _____

6. **bats:** plant eaters, blood eaters, fish eaters

    Principle of classification: _____

7. **burns:** first-degree, second-degree, third-degree

    Principle of classification: _____

8. **people:** U.S. citizens, permanent legal residents, illegal residents

    Principle of classification: _____

The Classification Essay

In your *classification essay*, once you have chosen a principle of classification, make sure that the classification includes all members of the group. For example, suppose you have decided to classify the students in your class by ethnicity. All the students fit nicely into the categories of Han, Zhuang, and Manchu except for one, who is Miao and does not fit. You must either add another category so that this student will fit or look for another principle of classification.

- To avoid omitting members, it's usually a good idea to divide the group into more than two categories. Most classification essays have three or four categories.

- In the thesis statement of a classification essay, introduce the categories of classification you will be using.

    EXAMPLES: People can be classified according to the shape of their chin: those who have a pointed chin, those who have a round chin, those who have a broad chin, and those who have a small chin.

    Wrinkles fall into two categories: horizontal and vertical.

    Fish fall into three basic classes: jawless fish, bony fish, and cartilaginous fish.

- When stating your categories in the thesis statement, remember to use parallel structure, or words of the same grammatical form, in the series.

    EXAMPLES: Teachers can be classified as those who dress formally, those who dress semiformally, and those who dress casually. (clauses)

    In terms of body language, people can be classified according to movements, posture, and facial expressions. (nouns)

    The Greeks categorized people as melancholic, phlegmatic, sanguine, and choleric. (adjectives)

Writing Practice

Write an Essay

Choose one of the following topics to write a classification essay.

1. Classifying a major type of food
2. Classifying the way people dress
3. Classifying your friends into three or four major categories

Pre-Write

A Use one of the pre-writing techniques you prefer (see Unit 2), and find a principle of classification that includes all the members of the group. Do not have more than five categories, since you need to write one paragraph for each category.

B Find an article that contains information on your topic and write a brief summary of it. Find a short excerpt from the article that you would like to include in your essay and paraphrase it (see Unit 3).

C Work on a thesis statement for your essay.

Organize Your Ideas

A Write your thesis statement using parallel structure.

B Identify each category, defining or describing it.

C Give examples and specific details for each category.

D Make a detailed outline, showing what will be in the Introduction, Body, and Conclusion.

Write a Rough Draft

Using your detailed outline and any notes you made in Pre-Write, write a rough draft of your essay.

Revise Your Rough Draft

Check the thesis statement, unity, development, coherence and purpose of your rough draft.

Edit Your Essay

Work with a partner or your teacher to edit your essay. Check the spelling, punctuation, vocabulary, and grammar.

Write Your Final Copy

After you edit your essay, you can write your final copy.

Translation

A Translate the following passage into English.

诞生于上世纪50年代的人体动作学（Kinesics）是一门新兴的学科，是研究人们在与他人谈话时通过肢体动作进行沟通的学科。我们所有人都会通过非言语的方式同他人交流，如通过手势和眉毛的变化来做敬礼的姿势，与他人目光相遇再移开，在椅子上变换位置。这些行为在我们看来都是随机无意的，但人体动作学专家近年来发现，这些肢体动作与语言一样，是一个连续一致且可以理解的系统。肢体语言亦具有区域文化特色，研究者有时可以通过说话时眉毛的变化来认出说话者的民族背景和社会阶层。

B Translate the following passage into Chinese.

In the West, parents tell their children "to follow the head, not the heart" and "not to be absent-minded while learning", whereas in China since ancient times, there have been sayings such as "The heart is the very organ generating thought" and "All wishes, from the bottom of one's heart, may come true" today. Where is thinking taking place then—in the brain or in the heart? In fact, scientifically speaking, "heart" in Western medicine and xin (heart) in traditional Chinese medicine are not the same thing. The former is a biological concept based on anatomy, biology and neurology while the latter is the "dwelling place of the spirit" filled with connotations of culture, philosophy, religion and even metaphysics, which are far beyond the domain of medicine. Therefore, the way to grasp the essence of "brain" and "heart" should not be confined to a scientific approach; rather it ought to be viewed cross-culturally. Otherwise, certain issues can be beyond comprehension.

Weaving It Together

Unit Project

Do research among your classmates. Interview them and collect information about their character and personality, their physical characteristics, and their lifestyle and living habits. Then report back to your classmates on your classification analysis. The following topics can be referred to:

1. Classifying character and personality of your friends
2. Classifying physical characteristics of your friends
3. Classifying lifestyle and living habits of your friends

Searching the Internet

A Search the Internet for information about personality theories. Find additional theories about the classification of personalities (for example, type A and type B; Carl Jung's Psychological Types; David Keirsey's "temperament sorter"; Katherine Benziger's Brain Type Theory). Find answers to these questions:

1. How many groups are the personalities classified into?
2. What are the personality types based on?

B Search for a "free personality test" on the Internet. What type of personality do you have, according to the test? Share the information with your classmates.

C You may use your research later to write a classification essay.

What Do You Think Now?

Refer to the very beginning of this unit. Do you know the answers now? Complete the sentence, or circle the best answer.

1. There (is/isn't) proof that the shape of your body and your character are connected.
2. Muscular people (are/are not) always dominant.
3. Introverts (are/aren't) more responsive to caffeine than extraverts.
4. _____ do not like crowded social gatherings.

Broadening Your Horizon

A

10 Ways Psychology Can Help You Live a Better Life

How can psychology apply to your everyday life? Do you think that psychology is just for students, academics, and therapists? Then think again. Because psychology is both an applied and a theoretical subject, it can be utilized in a number of ways.

B

How Subtle Eye Signals Help Turn-Taking in Conversation

In every conversation, there is an unspoken code—a set of social rules that guides you. When to talk, when to stop talking, when to listen, and where to look. But what happens to people with aphasia, a communication disorder that can occur after a stroke, brain injury or tumor, causing patients to make mistakes and misunderstand language?

C

How Your Face Shows Happy Disgust

We smile when we're happy. But how does a face strike the proper look to show, say, happy surprise? Or happy disgust, like when you're laughing at a really gross joke? A new report, published on Monday in the Proceedings of the National Academy of Sciences, shows that we instinctively mix and match actions from the six basic emotions to stitch together more subtle expressions.

UNIT 5
Gender

A female lion (on the left) and a male lion (on the right) in the Okavango Delta, Botswana

WHAT DO YOU THINK?

Answer these questions with your best guess. Circle *Yes* or *No*.

1. Do men talk more than women? Yes   No
2. Do women send more emails than men do? Yes   No
3. Do boys think their lives would improve if they were girls? Yes   No
4. Are there more men than women in the field of education? Yes   No

Reading 1

Pre-Reading

Preparing for the Reading Topic

A Discuss these questions with your classmates.

1. What are some ways in which males and females think and act differently?

2. Do you think boys and girls are born different or taught to be different?

3. Do you think most people have set ideas about male and female characteristics? How about you?

B Which of these stereotypes are commonly associated with men and which with women? Write *M* in the blank if you think it is a trait characteristic of men. Write *F* in the blank if you think it is a characteristic of women.

_____ 1. aggressive

_____ 2. ambitious

_____ 3. dependent

_____ 4. direct

_____ 5. gentle

_____ 6. logical

_____ 7. self-confident

_____ 8. tactful

_____ 9. talkative

_____ 10. unemotional

Key Vocabulary

As you read "Males and Females: What's the Difference?", pay attention to the following words and phrases and see if you can work out their meanings from the contexts.

resounding	status
come up with	Internet postings
make their point	adversarial
spatial	put-downs
bring about	sarcasm

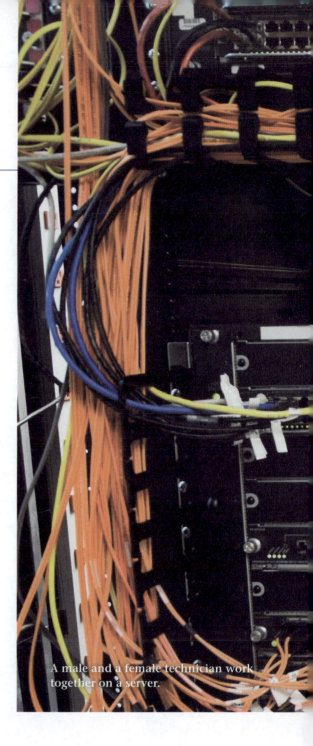

A male and a female technician work together on a server.

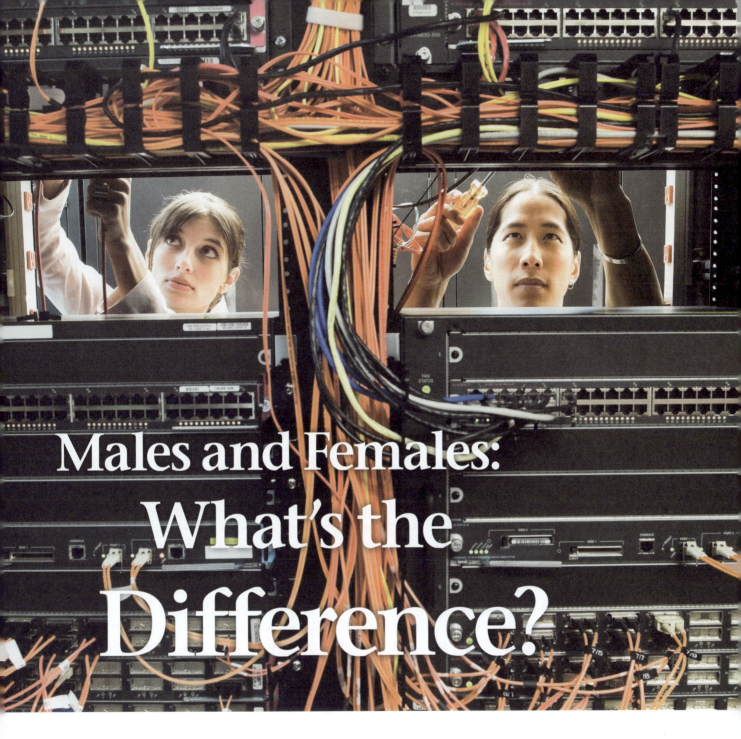

Males and Females: What's the Difference?

1   Is it true that men don't ask for directions? Do women talk more than men? Are men more jealous than women? Who likes the color red? Is there more to the difference between males and females than that meets the eye? The answers are *yes*, *no*, *yes*, *males*, and a **resounding** *yes*! Of course, these are generalizations. They don't apply to all men or all women. However, after decades of study, scientists and researchers have concluded that there are important differences in the way males and females think, speak, and act; in their values and habits; in what makes them laugh and what makes them cry. And they know that these differences are true across countries, cultures, ages, and other factors.

2   Does this sound like something you've known all along? It may, but not everyone has agreed with that. Over the years, there have been varying opinions on this subject. In the 1960s and 1970s, when women were fighting for equality, many people said that males

and females were not different beyond the physical. They gave dolls to boys and trucks to girls. They said that society taught girls and boys to behave differently. In one way, they were right. Males and females are basically alike. We're all human, after all. And society certainly does affect our thinking and behavior. Nevertheless, researchers now know that there are distinct differences between males and females that are not just social. They know for sure that not only are men's and women's brains different but that they use their brains differently as well!

3 If you think that boys and girls are different from birth, you're right. From the time they're born, boys and girls differ in the way they function and the way their brain works. Boy babies are more interested in objects than in people. Girl babies respond to the human voice more than boys do. At play, little girls naturally practice carrying infants. On the other hand, little boys play more actively and aggressively. Researchers agreed a long time ago that girls have better language abilities than boys. But now they know that it's all in their heads—that is, their brains. Both areas of the brain that deal with language work harder in girls than in boys. Also, girls use different parts of the brain when performing language tasks. Boys, however, are better at solving technical problems and have better math skills.

4 Recently, scientists and researchers have **come up with** a number of interesting differences between males and females. These differences are in ways as simple as color preferences and as complicated as memory. If you're a female who likes pink or a male who likes yellow, you won't be surprised to hear that it comes naturally. As it turns out, men prefer bright-colored things like yellow and red, whereas women prefer soft colors like pink and aqua[1]. But if you've always thought that women talk more than men, you're wrong. Most men probably wouldn't agree with this statement. But after decades of study, research has shown that men talk more than women overall. And while a woman talks to create a relationship with the listener, men, on the other hand, try to influence the listener. Men, it seems, are always trying to **make their point**! And they probably think they're right, too, because men are more self-assured, more self-centered, and more satisfied with their performance than women. Women are more critical of themselves and less self-assured. But all that self-doubt doesn't seem to make them sick. While women worry more about their health, men actually get sick twice as often. As to who is more forgiving, studies show that men are more vengeful and less forgiving than women. That's in spite of the fact that a woman is more likely to remember the wrongdoing! Whereas women are better at remembering faces and events, men can remember more symbolic and **spatial** things, such as how to find their way back from a place they've driven to. It's amusing to think about how some of these studies have proven what men and women have known all along. While men are better at finding their way or fixing a car, women are better at fixing friendships.

5 One of the biggest ways in which men and women are different is in how they communicate. Girls use language to get closer to others, to make friends. Language is used in a cooperative way. However, boys use language to establish their position among others. Language is used for competition. Both males and females carry these ways of using language into adulthood. This is true for all situations: in the home, at work, in

---

1 aqua 浅绿色的，水绿色的

personal and formal situations, in meetings, or at social functions. Women cooperate to **bring about** understanding. In contrast, men use power to negotiate their **status**. Recently, researchers were surprised to discover that this difference carries over into email communication and **Internet postings** in chat rooms.

6   At first, researchers thought that language differences would be less or even disappear in an Internet environment. After all, there's no physical interaction. Writers don't hear or see one another. So the playing field is quite equal. But as it turned out, they discovered that women and men have very different online ways of communicating. And these ways reflect exactly how they use language in their lives.

7   The language of males is **adversarial**. They use **put-downs**, like "Get a life," or "You must be dreaming!" or "Have you lost it?" They make strong statements, too: "It's a fact that… ," or "Here's what I know." They send more emails than women and they're longer. Men also use language that is self-promoting, such as, "I happen to be an expert on this subject." And they often use **sarcasm**, like "Yeah, right," or "Sure, and the moon's made of cheese."

8   On the other hand, females generally use language that is supportive, like "I'm sure you can do it." They express gratitude, such as, "Thanks for all your much-appreciated help," or "Thanks so much for the great advice." Not only do women apologize more, such as, "I'm sorry I haven't been in touch," or "I apologize if I sounded harsh," but they also express doubt and make self-conscious statements, like "I'm not sure I'm right about this, but…" Women ask more questions. And when they offer an idea or opinion, it's usually in the form of a suggestion, such as, "I think it might help you if… ," or "I suggest you…"

9   After extensive study, researchers have concluded that all in all, men use language that is aggressive, competitive, and dominating, whereas women offer support and friendship. Furthermore, they believe that the different ways in which men and women use language in emails is a result of their different goals. Men see Internet technology as a way to influence others and extend their authority and respect. On the other hand, women use it to strengthen existing friendships and make new ones.

10 Men and women have always known they are different. Men have thought long and hard about that, just as women have. It's what brings them together—and also gives them headaches! Knowing that boys and girls learn and communicate differently helps educators to teach more effectively. And, of course, knowing how the male and female brains differ can help everyone to understand each other better.

Vocabulary

Vocabulary in Context

A What are the meanings of the **bold** words or phrases? Circle the letter of the best answer.

1. The answers are *yes, no, yes, males*, and a **resounding** *yes*!
   - **a.** deep
   - **b.** loud
   - **c.** exciting
   - **d.** demanding

2. Scientists and researchers have **come up with** a number of interesting differences.
   - **a.** created
   - **b.** determined
   - **c.** furnished
   - **d.** designed

3. Men, it seems, are always trying to **make their point**!
   - **a.** assert their ideas and opinions
   - **b.** give purpose to their actions
   - **c.** give directions to a place
   - **d.** hold others to blame

4. Men can remember more symbolic and **spatial** things.
   - **a.** in a physical location
   - **b.** in a period of time
   - **c.** in the attitude
   - **d.** in the mind or imagination

5. Women cooperate to **bring about** understanding.
   - **a.** suggest
   - **b.** take on
   - **c.** prevent
   - **d.** cause

6. Men use power to negotiate their **status**.
   - **a.** duty or occupation
   - **b.** ability or talent
   - **c.** character or personality
   - **d.** rank or position

7. This difference carries over into email communication and **Internet postings**.
   - **a.** personal communications between two people on the Internet
   - **b.** statements put on the Internet for everyone to read
   - **c.** work-related statements among workers on company computers
   - **d.** government-controlled information on the Internet

8. The language of males is **adversarial**.
   - **a.** supportive
   - **b.** uncertain
   - **c.** competitive
   - **d.** friendly

9. They use **put-downs**.
   - **a.** statements meant to confuse
   - **b.** statements meant to shame
   - **c.** statements meant to be helpful
   - **d.** statements meant to entertain

10. Men often use **sarcasm** in their language.
    - **a.** words that are meaningless
    - **b.** words that are funny
    - **c.** words that make fun or insult
    - **d.** words that are reasonable

B Answer these questions with complete sentences.

1. How often do you make **Internet postings**?

2. What new invention in technology would you like someone to **come up with**?

3. What change would you like to **bring about** in society?

4. When might you hear a **resounding** applause?
_____

5. What is considered a **status** symbol?
_____

C Now write your own sentences. Use the following words or phrases in the sentences: **spatial**, **put-downs**, **sarcasm**, **adversarial**, and **make their point**.

_____
_____
_____

Vocabulary Building

A A compound adjective is often made by joining a past participle, or adjective ending in *-ed*, to another word using a hyphen, such as *a level-headed woman*. Complete these sentences, using compound adjectives from the reading.

1. A person who is concerned only with his own wants and needs is self-_____.
2. If you recognize something for its good qualities, it is much-_____.
3. A person who is nervous because he thinks everyone is looking at him is self-_____.
4. A person who is confident because he is sure of his own abilities is self-_____.
5. Things with strong, noticeable colors are bright-_____.
6. People who are trying to be more important are self-_____.

B Complete these sentences with the words you found in Exercise A.

1. Women often doubt themselves and are less _____ than men.
2. Men like _____ things, whereas women prefer softer colors.
3. Men often only think of themselves and are _____.
4. Women use phrases for thankfulness, such as "Your help was _____."
5. Men use _____ language to show they are experts and know everything.
6. Women are often _____ and not confident about the way they look.

Reading Comprehension

A Circle the letter of the best answer.

1. Paragraph 2 is mainly about the fact that _____.

   a. gender differences are mainly due to the way men's and women's brains are formed and function

   b. gender differences are mainly due to society influence

   c. males and females are basically alike

   d. there have been varying opinions on gender differences

2. Which of the following can best summarize the main idea of Paragraph 4?

   a. Men prefer bright colors, whereas women prefer soft colors.

   b. Research findings have provided many differences between men and women.

   c. Men talk more than women overall.

   d. Men are more vengeful and less forgiving than women.

3. The writer states that both males and females _____.

   a. change the way they use language as they get older

   b. carry their use of language into adulthood

   c. use language in the same ways

   d. use their brains in the same way when processing language

4. Researchers have reached the conclusion that in general, men use language that _____.

   a. is aggressive and competitive   b. is supportive of others

   c. makes and strengthens friendships   d. shows respect

5. It can be inferred from the reading that _____.

   a. men talk more than women in most situations

   b. differences in language use don't change in an Internet setting

   c. women offer their ideas and opinions in the form of suggestions

   d. women are more likely to remember the details of their best friend's wedding

B Complete the summary below using the list of words in the box.

forgive	vengeful	innate	researchers	sarcasm
ambitious	spatial	function	resounding	wrongdoing
status	dependent	overall	self-assured	adversarial

The differences between men and women are not learned, but are 1. _____, and these differences may be due to the different ways men's and women's brains 2. _____. Recently, scientists and 3. _____ have come up with some interesting differences between males and females, such as men prefer bright colors; men talk more than women 4. _____; men are more 5. _____, more self-centered and more self-satisfied; women tend to 6. _____ others more; men are better at remembering more symbolic and 7. _____ things. One of the biggest differences lies in language used to communicate. Women use language in a cooperative way to bring about understanding while men use it in a competitive way to negotiate their 8. _____. This difference extends into Internet communication as a result of different goals as well. Generally, men use language that is 9. _____ and they often use 10. _____, whereas women use language that is supportive. Knowing these differences between men and women and how their brains differ can not only help educators to teach effectively but also help everyone to understand each other better.

Critical Thinking

Discuss these questions with your classmates.

1. Do you think that ideas about what men and women are like have changed over time? If yes, give examples of how they have changed and note whether the changes have been positive or negative for each gender. If no, explain why they haven't changed and if that is good or bad.

2. How can stereotypes about males and females negatively affect a child's life? Can they have a positive effect as well? How?

3. What can men and women learn from the differences between them?

4. How has technology affected the way males and females think and act? Do you think there are fewer differences between males and females now than 200 years ago? Why or why not? What changes do you think will come in the future?

5. If you could create the "perfect" male and female, what character traits would they have, and why?

Reading 2

Pre-Reading

Preparing for the Reading Topic

A Discuss these questions with your classmates.

1. What are some choices in life that males and females make on the basis of gender?

2. What are some traditional rules of behavior for males and females? Do you think the rules are changing today? Why, or why not?

3. In the past, what kind of uncomfortable clothing did women wear to be fashionable? What uncomfortable clothing did men wear? Do you think this happened more in the past than it does in the present? Why, or why not?

B Which of these jobs are commonly associated with men and which with women? Write *M* in the blank if you think it is a job that more men do. Write *F* in the blank if you think it is a job more women do.

_____ 1. teacher

_____ 2. engineer

_____ 3. computer technician

_____ 4. social worker

_____ 5. mechanic

_____ 6. librarian

_____ 7. nurse

_____ 8. architect

_____ 9. scientist

_____ 10. software developer

Key Vocabulary

As you read "Life Chances", pay attention to the following words and see if you can work out their meanings from the contexts.

probability	criteria
aspect	viable
restricted	reject
conscious	dominated
ideals	admit

Life Chances

The following article is from Seeing Sociology *by Joan Ferrante[1], published in 2014.*

1   Sociologists define life chances as the **probability** that an individual's life will turn out a certain way. Life chances apply to virtually every **aspect** of life—the chances that a person will become an airline pilot, play T-ball[2], major in elementary education, spend an hour or more getting ready for work or school, or live a long life.

2   Sociologists are interested in the processes by which being male or female increases the probability that a person's life will be a certain way. Ideas about what men and women should be shape every aspect of life, including how people dress, the time they wake up in the morning, what they do after they wake up, the social rules they take on, the things they worry about, and even ways of expressing emotion and experiencing sexual attraction (Bem[3] 1993).

3   To understand the power of gender in shaping life chances, consider the now classic research by Alice Baumgartner-Papageorgiou[4] (1982) on elementary and high school students. She asked them how their lives would be different if they were the other gender. Their responses reflected culturally conceived and learned ideas about sex-appropriate behaviors and appearances and about the imagined and real advantages and disadvantages of being male or female (Vann[5] 1995). The boys generally believed that their life chances would change in negative ways if they became girls. Among other things, they would become less active and more **restricted** in what they could do. In addition, they would become more **conscious** about tending to their appearance, finding a husband, and being alone and unprotected in the face of a violent attack—"I'd use a lot of makeup and look good and beautiful" and "I would not be able to help my dad fix the car and his two motorcycles" (2–9).

4   The girls, on the other hand, believed that if they became boys they would be less emotional, their lives would be more active and less restrictive, they would be closer to their fathers, and they would be treated as more than "sex objects"—"My father would be closer, because I'd be the son he always wanted" and "People would take my decisions and beliefs more seriously" (5–13).

5   Baumgartner-Papageorgiou's findings about how one's life is shaped by gender seem to hold up across time. When I asked my students how their lives would change if they were the other gender, their responses were remarkably similar to those described above. Decisions about how early to get up in the morning, which subjects to study, whether to show emotion, how to sit, and what sports to play are influenced by society's **ideals** of

---

1 Joan Ferrante 琼·费兰特，美国北肯塔基大学社会学教授
2 T-ball 儿童棒球
3 Bem 贝姆（Sandra Ruth Lipsitz Bem）(1944–2014)，美国心理学家
4 Alice Baumgartner-Papageorgiou 爱丽丝·鲍姆加特纳-帕帕耶奥尔尤，美国科罗拉多大学教育平等研究所教授
5 Vann 范恩（Elizabeth D. Vann），美国北卡罗来纳大学教授

masculinity and femininity rather than by **criteria** such as self-fulfillment, interest, ability, or personal comfort.

6   When selecting a college major, many students consider, even if subconsciously, the "sex" of the major: if a major matches their sex, they consider the major to be a **viable** option, and if it does not match, they may **reject** the major outright (Bem 1993). Note that about 85 percent of bachelor's degrees in engineering and in computer-information sciences are awarded to males, whereas 94 percent of bachelor's degrees in library sciences are awarded to females. Other majors **dominated** by women include education, health professions, and public administration/social services. Approximately 80 percent of all bachelor's degrees awarded in these fields go to women (National Center for Education Statistics[6] 2011a).

7   Life chances include not just the probability of choosing a college major based on whether it is viewed as sex-appropriate but also the probability of wearing uncomfortable clothing. One study by the Society of Chiropodists[7] and Podiatrists[8] found that 40 percent of women **admit** to buying shoes that they know do not fit—that is, they are too narrow (by design) or too small by one or two sizes (Harris[9] 2003). This finding suggests that many women decide to wear uncomfortable shoes so they can appear more fashionable. Apparently, 17 percent of men buy shoes they know don't fit (BBC[10] 2009). It is not known whether men buy shoes that are larger or smaller than needed.

---

6 National Center for Education Statistics （美国）国家教育统计中心

7 chiropodist 手足病医生（尤指足病医生）

8 podiatrist 足病医生

9 Harris 哈里斯（Gardiner Harris），《纽约时报》的公共卫生记者

10 BBC 英国广播公司

Liu Yang, China's first female astronaut, waves to well-wishers as she prepares to depart on her space mission in June 2012.

Vocabulary

A What are the meanings of the **bold** words or phrases? Circle the letter of the best answer.

1. Sociologists define life chances as the **probability** that an individual's life will turn out a certain way.

    a. doubt
    b. certainty
    c. reason
    d. likelihood

2. Life chances apply to virtually every **aspect** of life.

    a. problem or concern
    b. task or responsibility
    c. element or condition
    d. time period

3. Boys generally believed they would be more **restricted** in what they could do.

    a. uncontrolled
    b. free
    c. careless
    d. limited

4. They would become more **conscious about** tending to their appearance.

    a. feeling bad about
    b. having one's mind on
    c. being unaware of
    d. not caring about

5. Decisions are influenced by society's **ideals of** masculinity and femininity.

    a. perfect ideas of
    b. common traits of
    c. sensible ideas about
    d. hopeful wishes for

6. Decisions are influenced by society's ideals of masculinity and femininity rather than by **criteria** such as self-fulfillment or personal comfort.

    a. beliefs based on faith
    b. standards for judgment
    c. proven points
    d. imaginary ideas

7. If a major matches their sex, they consider the major to be a **viable** option.

    a. temporary
    b. possible
    c. unsuitable
    d. questionable

8. If it does not match their sex, they may **reject** the major outright.

    a. give thought to
    b. receive willingly
    c. refuse to accept
    d. make room for

9. Other majors **dominated by** women include education and health professions.

    a. having the greatest number in
    b. having the least control over
    c. having the best choice of
    d. having a usual position in

10. Forty percent of women **admit** to buying shoes that they know do not fit.

    a. make up a story
    b. give an opinion
    c. state the truth
    d. start an argument

B Answer these questions with complete sentences.

1. What is something your parents **restricted** you from doing when you were young?
   _____

2. What **aspect** of your life do you enjoy the most?
   _____

3. What **criteria** do you use in selecting a restaurant in which to eat?
   _____

4. What is the **probability** that you will travel a long distance in the near future?
   _____

5. In your mind, what is an **ideal** teacher?
   _____

C Now write your own sentences. Use the following words in the sentences: *dominated*, *conscious*, *admit*, *reject*, and *viable*.

_____

_____

_____

Reading Comprehension

A Circle the letter of the best answer.

1. Which of the following statements is the main idea of the reading?

   a. Life chances apply to virtually every aspect of life.

   b. Gender exerts a great influence on selecting a college major.

   c. Gender affects both major and everyday decisions in our lives.

   d. Gender shapes one's life chances.

2. The boys generally believed that their life chances would _____ if they became girls.

   a. be less emotional   b. change in negative ways

   c. be more active   d. be less restrictive

3. _____ of bachelor's degree in engineering and in computer-information sciences are rewarded to males.

   a. 85%   b. 94%

   c. 80%   d. 40%

4. It can be inferred from the reading that _____.

   a. there are few, if any, areas of our lives not influenced by gender

   b. gender has influence over the least important aspects of our lives

   c. there's very little connection between gender and major life decisions

Unit 5 Gender 119

d. gender is only one small aspect of all the things that influence our lives

5. From the reading, it can be concluded that _____.

   a. young people's ideas about gender have changed greatly over the years

   b. today's young people consider any career open to them

   c. today's young people don't know what they want to do in the future

   d. gender ideals are so deep-rooted that they don't change much over time

B Find information in the reading to answer these questions. Note the number of paragraph where you find the answer. Discuss your answers with a partner.

1. Why is the research by Alice Baumgartner-Papageorgiou on elementary and high school students cited in the reading?

   _____
   _____

   Paragraph: _____

2. What influences our everyday decisions, such as how early to get up in the morning, which subjects to study, whether to show emotion, how to sit, and what sports to play?

   _____
   _____

   Paragraph: _____

3. What do many students consider when selecting a college major?

   _____
   _____

   Paragraph: _____

Critical Thinking

Discuss these questions with your classmates.

1. What do you think are the advantages and disadvantages of being male or female?

2. If you had been born a different gender, how do you think your life would be different right now?

3. What is gender discrimination? What are some common phenomena of gender discrimination in society, the workplace, and in schools? How can gender discrimination affect males and females respectively?

4. Besides gender, what are some other things that determine your life chances?

5. How much control do you think you have over your lives? What are some life chances that you can control or cannot? What aspects of your life do you feel have already been predetermined?

Writing

Writing Skills

How to Quote

In academic writing, you are expected to support your ideas to make them convincing to the reader. Writing about your own experience alone will not often convince people. If you can refer to a newspaper story, magazine article, or book in which an authority agrees with you, your ideas will have more weight.

- The best way to use quoted material is to integrate it into your own writing. You should begin by saying something about the subject in your own words. Then use the quotation to explain the significance of your statement.

    EXAMPLE:
    Often gender stereotyping gets passed down from one generation to another, even if the parents themselves don't adhere to such beliefs. In their article "Gender Stereotypes and Parenting", Dr. Kathleen Moritz Rudasill and Dr. Carolyn M. Callahan state, "As parents, we have a significant role in nurturing our children's interests, values and, ultimately, career decisions. Often, we unintentionally introduce gender stereotypes (beliefs about acceptable roles for boys or girls) through our interactions with our children or introduce gender stereotype thinking into the home" (2008, National Association for Gifted Children, Updated on April 23, 2014).

- The rules for quoting are as follows.
    1. Put a comma after the introductory, or *stating* phrase. Put quotation marks before and after the words quoted. Capitalize the first word of the quotation if it is the start of a sentence in the original material.

        EXAMPLE: They report, "Although both mothers and fathers have an impact on children's career development, mothers may be more influential than fathers, teachers, and even peers."

    2. If the quotation is broken, put quotation marks around both parts and separate the parts with commas. Do not begin the second part with a capital letter unless it is a new sentence.

        EXAMPLE: "Although both mothers and fathers have an impact on children's career development," they report, "mothers may be more influential than fathers, teachers, and even peers."

- **Omitting words.** It is important to use the exact words of the author you are quoting. If you have to omit part of a quotation to fit the context of your writing, use an *ellipsis*, which is three spaced periods (...).

    EXAMPLE: Drs. Rudasill and Callahan write, "... our beliefs affect our behaviors, which in turn influence children's development of self-concept, interests, and career goals" ("Gender Stereotypes and Parenting").

- **Adding words.** If you need to add words to the original quotation in order to explain it or to make it fit into the structure of your writing, put square brackets [ ] around the words you've added.

    EXAMPLE: "High school juniors [15 to 17 years old] report that they talk more to their mothers than anyone else about their career plans and the training and education needed for a career," Rudasill and Callahan stated.

- **Reporting words.** To introduce a quotation, reporting verbs such as the ones below may be used. Note that the person being quoted may be introduced by the word *as*.

    As Rudasill and Callahan **said**, "..."   As they **declared**, "..."
    As they **stated**, "..."   As they **maintained**, "..."
    As they **reported**, "..."   As they **insisted**, "..."
    As they **wrote**, "..."

- Reporting verbs and phrases without the word *as* can be used in the present or past tense.

    Rudasill and Callahan **said**, "..."   They **further stated**, "..."
    They **believe**, "..."   They **continued**, "..."

    EXAMPLES: Rudasill and Callahan **further stated**, "Our values also influence the particular interests, developed competencies, and self-concepts our children cultivate, and these characteristics are important indicators of career choice."

    "If we show that we place a high value on science ability," they **continued**, "then our children are likely to be interested in science, feel confident in their science abilities, and take advanced courses in that subject."

- Use the phrase *according to...* only when you are paraphrasing (see Unit 3). Do not use *according to...* when citing with quotation marks.

    EXAMPLES: **According to** the International Labor Organization, between 1980 and 2009, the global rate of female labor force participation rose from 50.2 percent to 51.8 percent, while the male rate fell from 82.0 percent to 77.7 percent.

    Between 1980 and 2009, the global rate of female labor force participation rose from 50.2 percent to 51.8 percent, while the male rate fell from 82.0 percent to 77.7 percent, **according to** the International Labor Organization.

- Remember *always* to document the source of your quotation, even when it is not a direct quotation. If you don't document the source, you will be guilty of plagiarism. *Plagiarism* is using other people's words or ideas without acknowledging the source of that information. It is wrong to use another person's work without giving credit; if you do this in an assignment or in an examination, you may be disqualified from receiving a grade. Therefore, you must always use quotation marks and cite your source when you use someone's exact words. You must cite your source when you paraphrase.

Exercise 1

Decide if the following sentences have Correct Punctuation (*CP*) or Incorrect Punctuation (*IP*). Then correct the sentences.

_____ 1. As they wrote in the *World Bank Report*, "... despite significant progress in female labor force participation over the past 25 years, pervasive and persistent gender differences remain in productivity and earnings across different sectors and jobs."

_____ 2. As stated in their most recent report, "promoting decent and productive employment and income opportunities equally for women and men is one of the key priorities of the ILO's International Labor Organization] Decent Work Agenda.

_____ 3. "For instance, they further stated, "Women are more likely than men to work in jobs that offer flexible working arrangements [such as part-time or informal jobs) so that they can combine work with care responsibilities" (*World Bank Report*).

_____ 4. As Margaret Thatcher once said, "In politics, if you want anything said, ask a man. If you want anything done, ask a woman."

_____ 5. Men marry women with the hope they will never change. Women marry men with the hope they will change," asserted Albert Einstein, adding, "invariably they are both disappointed.

_____ 6. In his book *Life Is Worth Living*, Fulton J. Sheen wrote, "The difference between the love of a man and the love of a woman is that a man will always give reasons for loving, but a woman gives no reasons for loving."

_____ 7. Drs. Rudasill and Callahan declare "…as parents who support and advise our children's career development, we pave the way for our children to feel free to pursue non-traditional careers, such as engineering or computer science for girls, and music or elementary school teaching for boys—or not!

Exercise 2

Paraphrase each of the following quotes, using the phrase *according to…*

1. In her article "Girls Are… Boys Are…: Myths, Stereotypes & Gender Differences", Patricia B. Campbell states, "There is a lot of talk about 'sex differences' and a lot of research and writing as well. The reality is that girls as a group and boys as a group are more alike than they are different" (1994).

   _____
   _____
   _____

2. As Campbell reports in her article "Girls Are… Boys Are…: Myths, Stereotypes & Gender Differences", "When hundreds of studies of math-related skills are examined and summarized, as the following graph shows, there is almost a complete overlap between the scores of girls as a group and the scores of boys as a group" (1994).

   _____
   _____
   _____

3. "Globally, economic development has been accompanied by growing economic opportunities for women (particularly in manufacturing and services)," states the International Labor Organization report.

   _____
   _____
   _____

4. "*Pink is for girls* is a recent idea," asserts J.F. Sargent in his article "5 Gender Stereotypes That Used To Be the Exact Opposite." He adds, "For most families, finding out the gender of their baby early on is crucial, since everyone needs to know what color of clothes and toys to get them—pink or blue? Almost immediately after being born, an infant is outfitted with his or her uniform (a blue T-shirt or pink headband, respectively) so there can be no confusion" (April 24, 2012).

   _____
   _____
   _____

Comparison and Contrast

Comparison and contrast is a very useful and common method of essay organization. Many college essay assignments require you to compare and contrast ideas, theories, facts, characters, principles, and so on. In your personal life, too, you find similarities and differences in a whole array of things, from the products you buy to the friends you make and the jobs you get.

- When you *compare* two items, you show how aspects of one item are *similar* to aspects of another. A comparison tells you what features are similar.

- When you *contrast* two items, you show the differences between them. You point out the features that are not alike or are *different*.

- **Finding two comparable items.** To make a comparison, you need to choose two items that share a similar feature or have the same function. In Reading 1, the ways men and women think, speak, and act are compared. In Reading 2, gender beliefs between male and female students are compared. It would not be a good idea to compare a male youth and a female adult. However, male and female youths or male and female adults could be compared and contrasted.

- **The basis of comparison.** The basis of comparison is an important aspect of the organization and development of a comparison-and-contrast essay. When comparing two items, you must compare the same aspects of each. For example, in comparing two people, the basis of comparison could be appearance, behavior, or personality. Whatever bases of comparison you choose, you must use the same ones to discuss each person. You cannot compare the personality of one person to the appearance of the other.

Exercise 3

Complete the column "Basis of Comparison" in the chart below, to show how two universities can be compared.

Basis of Comparison	University A	University B
1.	large	small
2.	rural	urban
3.	affordable	expensive
4.	emphasis on sciences	emphasis on the arts

Exercise 4

Work with a partner. Write the names of two examples for each group. Say how the examples can be compared.

1. fast-food restaurants   _____   _____
2. amusement parks   _____   _____
3. computers   _____   _____
4. cars   _____   _____

The Comparison-and-Contrast Essay

In a *comparison-and-contrast essay*, you may want to compare and contrast two items to show that one is better than the other, that the two are totally different, or that they have some similarities and some differences. Purposes will vary.

- **The thesis statement** for a comparison-and-contrast essay should include the names of the two items being compared and the dominant impression of each item.

    EXAMPLE: University A is a better choice for me than University B because of its size, location, reputation, and specialty.

- There are two basic ways to organize a comparison-and-contrast essay.
    1. Block organization
    2. Point-by-point organization

- In **block organization**, one item is discussed in one block (one or more paragraphs), and the other is discussed in another block. For example, imagine you were going to write a comparison-and-contrast essay about two male or female acquaintances or friends. The following outline shows how you might organize your essay using block organization.

    Block Organization Outline

    Topic: A comparison and contrast of two female best friends, Nancy and Karen

    Thesis Statement: Nancy and Karen are best friends and have similarities and differences in their looks, personality, and physical strength.

    I. Nancy
       A. Looks (tall, dark, strong)
       B. Personality (not afraid to talk, very friendly)
       C. Physical Strength (strong, plays sports with the boys)
    II. Karen
       A. Looks (not tall, blond, frail)
       B. Personality (afraid to talk, very shy)
       C. Physical Strength (not strong, afraid of any physical sports)

    Conclusion

- In **point-by-point organization**, similarities and differences on the same point are discussed together. The following outline shows how you might organize your essay using point-by-point organization.

    Point-by-Point Organization Outline

    Topic: A comparison and contrast of two female best friends, Nancy and Karen

    Thesis Statement: Nancy and Karen are best friends and have similarities and differences in their looks, personality, and physical strength.

    I. Looks
       A. Nancy (tall, dark, strong)
       B. Karen (not tall, blond, frail)
    II. Personality
       A. Nancy (not afraid to talk, very friendly)
       B. Karen (afraid to talk, very shy)
    III. Physical Strength
       A. Nancy (strong, plays sports with the boys)

B. Karen (not strong, afraid of any physical sports)

Conclusion

- As you can see, the block organization is simpler because fewer transitions are required and one subject is discussed completely before going on to the other. The point-by-point organization, in which similarities and differences of each point are discussed together, requires repeated use of comparison-and-contrast indicators.

Comparison-and-Contrast Indicators

A good comparison-and-contrast essay is sprinkled with *comparison-and-contrast indicators*, or structure words. The following is a list of some of these structure words, already mentioned in Unit 5, Book 2.

- **Comparison Indicators**

Sentence Connectors	Clause Connectors	Others
also	and	(be) similar to
likewise	as	(be) the same as
similarly	just as	both... and
		just like (+ noun)
		like (+ noun)
		not only... but also
		similar to (+ noun)

- **Contrast Indicators**

Sentence Connectors	Clause Connectors	Others
however	although	but
in contrast	even though	despite (+ noun)
nevertheless	whereas	different from (+ noun)
on the other hand	while	in spite of (+ noun)
on the contrary		yet

Exercise 5

Combine the two sentences using the comparison or contrast word indicated. Make any necessary changes. The first one is done for you.

1. **although**

    Most people think women talk more than men. Research has shown that men actually talk more than women overall.

    Although most people think women talk more than men, research has shown that men actually talk more than women overall.

2. **whereas**

    Boys use language for competition. Girls use language to make friendships.

3. **likewise**
   Gender studies help educators teach more effectively. Gender studies help doctors treat patients better.

   _____
   _____

4. **just as**
   Girls naturally practice carrying infants. Boys naturally play more aggressively.

   _____
   _____

5. **however**
   Males and females are basically alike. Researchers have found some real and distinct differences between the sexes.

   _____
   _____

6. **in contrast**
   The online language of males is adversarial. Females use language that is supportive.

   _____
   _____

7. **on the other hand**
   Men are good at remembering symbolic and spatial things. Women are good at remembering faces and events.

   _____
   _____

8. **while**
   Girls have an ability for language. Boys are good at solving technical problems.

   _____
   _____

9. **nevertheless**
   Society does influence the thinking and behavior of males and females. Research has shown that gender differences are not just social.

   _____
   _____

10. **on the contrary**
    Women use the Internet to strengthen or make new friendships. Men use Internet technology to influence others and extend their authority.

    _____
    _____

Writing Practice

Write an Essay

Choose one of the following topics to write a comparison-and-contrast essay.

1. Two people whom you know something about
2. The past and present of a place you know
3. The lifestyles, social status, and feelings toward each other of two groups of people in China

Pre-Write

A Use one of the pre-writing techniques you prefer (see Unit 2), and find your bases of comparison and supporting ideas.

B Find an article that contains information on your topic and write a brief summary of it (see Unit 4). Find a short excerpt from the article that you would like to include in your essay and paraphrase it (see Unit 3). Find one or two statements written by the author that you might like to quote in your essay.

C Work on a thesis statement for your essay.

Organize Your Ideas

A Write your thesis statement.

B Select three or four bases of comparison from your Pre-Write exercises.

C Give examples and specific details for each category.

D Make a detailed outline. Choose between the block and point-by-point organization.

Write a Rough Draft

Using your detailed outline and any notes you made in Pre-Write, write a rough draft of your essay.

Revise Your Rough Draft

Check the thesis statement, unity, development, coherence and purpose of your rough draft.

Edit Your Essay

Work with a partner or your teacher to edit your essay. Check the spelling, punctuation, vocabulary, and grammar.

Write Your Final Copy

After you edit your essay, you can write your final copy.

Translation

A Translate the following passage into English.

在中国，旧社会的女人附庸于男人，同时背负着"三从四德""男尊女卑"等封建道德枷锁。作为男人的私有财产，女人的主要责任就是取悦丈夫和生儿育女。1949年新中国成立以来，特别是随着中国经济的持续发展和社会的全面进步，中国妇女的地位发生了巨大的变化。男女平等的观念深入人心，妇女变得更加独立，她们就职于各级政府、经济、文化、教育和科学领域，占总劳动力的很大比例。在21世纪的今天，中国的女性确实撑起了半边天。

B Translate the following passage into Chinese.

There are high heels that come in a variety of styles, textures, and colors in department stores and closets all over the world. Their outward appearance seems rather appealing and most women believe that they are more beautiful or sophisticated for wearing heels. But the fact remains that wearing high heels is harmful to one's physical health. Talk to any podiatrist, and you will hear that the majority of their business comes from high-heel-wearing women. High heels are known to cause problems such as deformed feet and torn toenails. The risk of severe back problems and twisted or broken ankles is three times higher for a high heel wearer than for a flat shoe wearer. Wearing heels also creates the threat of getting a heel caught in a sidewalk crack or a sewer-grate and being thrown to the ground—possibly breaking a nose, back, or neck. And of course, after wearing heels for a day, any woman knows she can look forward to a night of pain as she tries to comfort her swollen, aching feet.

Weaving It Together

Unit Project

Conduct a survey among your male classmates and female classmates. Give a presentation of your survey results to your classmates. You may ask your classmates the following questions:

1. What do male and female students share in common?
2. How do male and female students think and act differently?
3. Do the stereotypes about males and females affect the life of a university student?
4. Is there any gender discrimination in your university?
5. What else can we learn from each other's differences in gender?

Searching the Internet

A Search the Internet or do your own survey of text and email messages among your friends, relatives, and acquaintances. Find the answers to these questions:

1. What special words do women use?
2. What type of language do men use?
3. Do men write to women in the same way as they do to men?
4. Do your findings agree with Reading 1?

B Search the Internet to look up "gender roles" in various countries. Find two or three points of comparison. Share the information with your classmates.

C You may use your research later to write a comparison-and-contrast essay.

What Do You Think Now?

Refer to the very beginning of this unit. Do you know the answers now? Complete the sentence, or circle the best answer.

1. Men (talk/don't talk) more than women.
2. Women (send/don't send) more emails than men do.
3. Boys think their lives would (improve/not improve) if they were girls.
4. There are more _____ in the field of education.

Broadening Your Horizon

A

Why Men and Women Can't Be "Just Friends"

Can men and women really be "just friends?" Is the idea of a pure, platonic relationship between non-related, heterosexual men and women a myth? For the most part, it would seem the answer is "yes" and the reason is deeply rooted in the evolutionary soil of our species.

B

The Science of Selfies: A Five-City Comparison

Where do people smile the most? The least? Who poses most expressively?

C

Man, Weeping

One of our most firmly entrenched ideas of masculinity is that men don't cry. However, history is full of sorrowful knights, sobbing monks and weeping lovers—what happened to the noble art of the manly cry?

UNIT 6
Nutrition

Pomegranates—their bright red seeds have been valued for centuries for their nutritional benefits.

WHAT DO YOU THINK?

Answer these questions with your best guess. Circle *Yes* or *No*.

1. Are artificial sweeteners not dangerous to our health? Yes No
2. Does the average American eat about five pounds of food additives per year? Yes No
3. Do people worry about the safety of genetically engineered foods? Yes No
4. Has a lot of research been done on the health effects of hormones in our food? Yes No

Reading 1

Pre-Reading

Preparing for the Reading Topic

A Discuss these questions with your classmates.

1. Why do food products have labels?
2. Do you know why it is important to read the labels on products?
3. Do people use additives in food in China?
4. How long do you think additives have been used in food?

B Match the food additive in the box to the food in which it would probably be found. Some additives are used more than once.

> a. ascorbic acid (stops natural ripening)
> b. aspartame (artificial sweetener)
> c. BHA (stops bacteria in high-fat foods)
> d. emulsifiers (keep oil and water mixed)
> e. potassium sorbate (inhibits the growth of mold)
> f. synthetic food dye
> g. sulfites (block bacterial growth that make food rancid)

_____ 1. bread
_____ 2. butter
_____ 3. cheese
_____ 4. cured meat
_____ 5. low-calorie soda
_____ 6. red licorice candy
_____ 7. salad dressing
_____ 8. sugarless chewing gum
_____ 9. tomato
_____ 10. yellow cake frosting

Key Vocabulary

As you read "What's *Really* on Your Dinner Plate?", pay attention to the following words and phrases and see if you can work out their meanings from the contexts.

mold	ingests
controversy	metabolize
fake	loaded with
contaminated	poses
preservative	residues

What's *Really* on Your Dinner Plate?

1 **W**hat's that on your pizza? You can bet it's not just the extra cheese and onions you ordered. As a matter of fact, you can count on at least a dozen other "extras" that you never asked

for, including dextrin[1], mono- and diglycerides[2], potassium bromate[3], sodium aluminum phosphate[4], sodium citrate[5], sodium metabisulfite[6], and xanthan gum[7]. These common food additives make your pizza—among other things—lighter, tastier, and generally more pleasing to the palate. Because we like our pepperoni without **mold**, our crackers crispy, our peanut butter smooth, and our tomatoes red, chemicals are added to just about everything we eat. They make food more flavorful and easier to prepare; they make it last longer, look more appetizing, and feel better in our mouths (no lumps!).

2   Today's additives read like a chemistry book, so many people believe they're a modern invention. However, additives are nothing new, and neither is the **controversy** surrounding them. London in the eighteenth century could have been called the "adulterated food capital of the world", though it's likely that other cities in other countries were just as guilty of the practice of food adulteration. One might think that food in the "old days" was pure and simple; but in many cases, what people paid for was not what they were getting. Pepper, for example, was adulterated with mustard husks[8], pea flour, fruit berries, and sweepings from the storeroom floor. Tea, which was very expensive and brought all the way from China, was mixed with dried leaves from ash trees[9]. China tea was green, so **fake** China tea was often made from dried thorn leaves[10] colored with a poisonous substance called *verdigris*[11]. When black Indian tea became popular, it was common for manufacturers to buy up used tea leaves, which they stiffened with a gum solution and then tinted with lead, another dangerous substance. Even candy was **contaminated** with highly poisonous salts of copper and lead to give it color. These practices eventually came to the public's attention, and in 1860 the first British Food and Drug Act was passed. Despite the regulations on food purity that currently exist in almost every country, there are still problems. One of the most alarming cases occurred in 1969, when an Italian gentleman was charged for selling what was supposed to be grated parmesan[12] cheese, but turned out to consist of grated umbrella handles!

3   Believe it or not, food adulteration is not all bad. Salt has been used as a **preservative** for thousands of years, and, thanks to some basic and other quite complicated substances, we have "fresh" vegetables in January, peanut butter that doesn't stick to the roof of the mouth, stackable potato chips, and meat that doesn't turn green on the way home from the grocery store. But as they say, there's a price to pay for everything.

---

1 dextrin 糊精
2 mono- and diglycerides 单酸甘油酯和双酸甘油酯
3 potassium bromate 溴酸钾
4 sodium aluminum phosphate 磷酸钠铝
5 sodium citrate 柠檬酸钠
6 sodium metabisulfite 焦亚硫酸钠
7 xanthan gum 黄原胶
8 mustard husk 芥末外壳
9 ash tree 白蜡树
10 thorn leaf 荆棘叶
11 verdigris 铜绿，铜锈
12 parmesan 帕尔马干酪

4   In the case of vegetables and fruits, the price is taste. Bred for looks and long hauls, plump, red tomatoes have fine body and perfect skin but offer very little for our taste buds to smile about. The reason is that the tomatoes are picked green and then "gassed" along the way; that is, they're treated with ethylene[13] gas, the same gas tomatoes give off internally if allowed to ripen on the vine. The artificial gassing tricks the tomatoes into turning red. They don't really ripen; they just turn a ripe color.

5   The federal government recognizes about 35 different categories of additives, which are used for various purposes. Antioxidants[14] are added to oil-containing foods to prevent the oil from spoiling. Chelating agents[15] stop food from discoloring. Emulsifiers[16] keep oil and water mixed together. Flavor enhancers improve the natural flavor of food. Thickening agents absorb some of the water present in food and make food thicker. They also keep oils, water, and solids well mixed. About 800 million pounds (363 million kilograms) of additives are added to our food every year.

6   What happens when we consume this conglomeration of chemicals? The average American **ingests** about five pounds (2.27 kilograms) of food additives per year. The good news is that the majority of the hundreds of chemicals that are added to food are safe. In some cases, they're even good for us, such as when vitamins are added. The bad news is that some of them are not safe, and these are the ones with which we need to concern ourselves.

7   The first of the unsafe additives is artificial sweeteners. The sugar substitute aspartame[17] is sold commercially as Equal®[18] or NutraSweet®[19] and is used in many diet beverages. However, studies have shown that about 1 out of 20,000 babies cannot **metabolize** 1 of the 2 substances that aspartame is made from and that toxic levels of that substance, called phenylalanine[20], can result in mental retardation. Some scientists also believe that aspartame can cause problems with brain function and behavior changes in people who consume it. Some people who have consumed aspartame have reported dizziness, headaches, and even seizures. Another controversy over aspartame involves its possible link to an increased risk of brain tumors. Aspartame is still widely added, although many lawsuits have been filed to block its use. Another sugar substitute, called saccharin, has been linked to cancer in laboratory animals.

8   The additives sodium nitrite[21] and sodium nitrate[22] are two closely related chemicals that have been used for centuries to preserve meat. These additives keep meat's red color, enhance its flavor, and stop the growth of dangerous bacteria. Nitrate by itself is harmless, but it is quickly changed into nitrite by a chemical reaction that occurs at high temperatures and may also occur to some degree in the stomach. During this chemical

---

13 ethylene 乙烯
14 antioxidant 抗氧化剂
15 chelating agent 螯合剂
16 emulsifier 乳化剂
17 aspartame 阿斯巴甜
18 Equal® 怡口糖（注册商品名）
19 NutraSweet® 纽特（注册商品名）
20 phenylalanine 苯基丙氨酸
21 sodium nitrite 亚硝酸钠
22 sodium nitrate 硝酸钠

reaction, nitrite combines with other chemicals to form some very powerful cancer-causing agents. Bacon is a special problem because it is thinly sliced and fried at a high temperature. Other processed meats, such as hot dogs, ham, and bologna, are less of a risk. Nitrite has been considered an important cause of stomach cancer in the United States, Japan, and other countries. In the United States, in fact, the rate of stomach cancer has been declining for a number of years because of reduced use of nitrite and nitrate preservatives.

9   Artificial colorings, often used in combination with artificial flavorings, replace natural ingredients that are more costly to produce. Lemon-flavored "lemonade" is much cheaper to make than a real lemon product. Artificial colorings are synthetic dyes such as Blue No. 1, Blue No. 2, Citrus Red No. 2[23], Green No. 3, Red No. 3, Red No. 40, Yellow No. 5, and Yellow No. 6. They are widely used in foods to make them look more natural and more attractive. All those colored breakfast cereals for kids are **loaded with** food dyes, as are ice cream, cakes, and other tasty treats. For decades, questions have been asked about the safety of synthetic food dyes, and many dyes have been banned for being toxic or cancer causing. There are still questions of safety about the dyes that are currently in use. Yellow No. 5, for example, causes allergic reactions in some people. Red No. 3 has been banned for some uses because it caused tumors in rats. Other dyes are also under investigation.

10   It's good to know that no single food additive **poses** a severe danger to the entire population. But several additives, such as those we have mentioned, do pose some risks to the general public and should be avoided as much as possible. Fortunately, people are more aware than ever of the dangers of pesticide **residues** on fruits and vegetables and of additives in our processed foods. There is intense pressure on the federal government to ban unsafe substances. But it is also our responsibility as consumers to read labels and be aware of what we're putting into our bodies, and to learn how to eat safe and healthy food for long and healthy lives.

Vocabulary

Vocabulary in Context

A What are the meanings of the **bold** words or phrases? Circle the letter of the best answer.

1. We like to have pepperoni without **mold**.

    a. yellow fat
    b. strange spices
    c. greenish growth
    d. reddish color

2. The **controversy** surrounding additives is nothing new.

    a. purpose
    b. debate
    c. idea
    d. judgment

3. **Fake** China tea was often made from dried thorn leaves colored with a poisonous substance.

---

23 Citrus Red No. 2 柑橘红2号

a. imitation
   b. cheap
   c. ordinary
   d. light

4. Even candy was **contaminated** with highly poisonous salts.
   a. injured
   b. destroyed
   c. diseased
   d. made impure

5. Salt has been used as a **preservative** for thousands of years.
   a. substance used to give food a nice color
   b. substance used to keep food fresh
   c. substance used to dry out meat
   d. substance used to make food taste better

6. The average American **ingests** about five pounds of additives per year.
   a. cleans in the body
   b. changes to liquid
   c. takes in as food
   d. discharges from the body

7. Studies have shown that some babies cannot **metabolize** one of the substances that aspartame is made from.
   a. change into energy
   b. grow with
   c. sleep with
   d. live on

8. All the colored breakfast cereals for kids are **loaded with** food dyes.
   a. made out of
   b. destroyed by
   c. improved with
   d. packed with

9. No single food additive **poses** a severe danger to the entire population.
   a. transmits
   b. maintains
   c. presents
   d. donates

10. People are aware of the dangers of pesticide **residues** on fruits and vegetables.
    a. remainders
    b. samples
    c. trash
    d. portions

B Answer these questions with complete sentences.

1. What do plants **metabolize** to make them grow?

2. What **residue** might a detective look for in a crime scene?

3. Other than food, where else may you find **mold**?

4. What might **pose** a risk to someone outside during a storm?

5. Why would someone want to buy a **fake** product?

C Now write your own sentences. Use the following words or phrases in the sentences: **loaded with**, **controversy**, **ingests**, **contaminated**, and **preservative**.

_____
_____
_____

Vocabulary Building

A Match each noun listed below to a Passive Verb Phrase and an Object to make sentences similar to those used in the reading. Draw lines between the Noun, Passive Verb Phrase, and Object as in the example. The first one is done for you.

Noun	Verb Phrase	Object
1. Chemicals	are added to	cancer.
2. Pepper	are loaded with	copper salts.
3. Tea	has been linked to	dried leaves.
4. Candy	was adulterated with	everything we eat.
5. Saccharin	was contaminated with	food dyes.
6. Breakfast cereals	was mixed with	mustard husks.

B Make a question out of each of the sentences in Exercise A. The first one is done for you.

1. *What is added to everything we eat?*
2. _____
3. _____
4. _____
5. _____
6. _____

Reading Comprehension

A Circle the letter of the best answer.

1. The main idea of Paragraph 2 is that _____.

   a. food additives are chemical substances

   b. some suppliers adulterate food to save money

   c. food adulteration has a long and sometimes dangerous history

   d. even something as innocent-looking as candy can be dangerous if it has additives

2. Paragraph 9 is mainly concerned with _____.

   a. the questionable safety of food dyes

   b. the money-saving value of artificial flavorings and colorings

   c. the banning of toxic and cancer-causing food dyes

   d. the most popular foods in which dyes are used

3. Why does the writer take bacon as a typical example in Paragraph 8?
   a. Because bacon is thinly sliced and easily turns into nitrate in high temperatures.
   b. Because nitrate that is in bacon can be easily changed into nitrite in high temperatures since bacon slices are thinly cut and fried.
   c. Because lots of chemicals that bacon has can be easily changed into sodium nitrite.
   d. Because bacon contains nitrite, which is harmful.

4. The reading implies that _____.
   a. today's food additives are more dangerous than those used in the past
   b. economics has always played a role in the use of food additives
   c. food additives have more to do with making food look good than anything else
   d. regulations on food safety have eliminated most problems with food adulteration

5. From the reading, it can be concluded that _____.
   a. the health risks posed by some additives must be weighed against their positive values, such as food preservation
   b. Americans gain weight as a result of the large amount of food additives they consume
   c. most food additives are bad for us and should be banned
   d. there is no evidence to prove that banning certain additives reduces the risk of cancer

B Complete the summary below using the list of words in the box.

stiffen	tastier	mold	manufacturers	tumors
metabolize	assume	contaminated	adulteration	season
mental	palate	conscious	artificial	allergic

In the reading, the author talks about food additives that are common in our daily life. They make our pizza lighter, **1.**_____, and more pleasing to the palate. Actually, in the old days food was not as pure and simple as we **2.**_____. For example, London in the 18th century could have been called the capital of the world of food **3.**_____. Since tea prevailed at that time, **4.**_____ used poisonous substances to give it colors. Even candy was **5.**_____ with highly poisonous salts of copper. However, food additives are not all bad. They enable us to have vegetables which are not in **6.**_____ and fresh meat that doesn't turn green on the way home.

But there is a price to pay for everything. One of the unsafe additives is artificial sweeteners. Studies have shown that such sugar substitutes can cause problems like **7.**_____ retardation and behavior changes in some people. Furthermore, research has confirmed that some food dyes can cause some **8.**_____ reactions in some people and **9.**_____ in rats. Fortunately, people are more **10.**_____ of the dangers of the chemical substances and additives in food. We should also have responsibility as consumers to care about what we're putting into our bodies.

Critical Thinking

Discuss these questions with your classmates.

1. What do the terms *health food* and *organic food* mean? What are the controversies surrounding the use of those terms?

2. Health-food stores seem to be popping up everywhere. Do you think these stores provide healthier foods for their customers? Why or why not?

3. What do you think would happen if all the chemicals were removed from foods?

4. How does your diet differ from that of your grandparents and great grandparents? How do you think people's diets will change in the future?

5. If you had a choice between (1) food that was more expensive and less appetizing but was healthy and (2) food that was nice-looking and appetizing but was chemically treated, which would you choose and why?

Reading 2

Pre-Reading

Preparing for the Reading Topic

A Discuss these questions with your classmates.

1. Do you think that genetically engineered foods are safe? Why or why not?

2. Do you think that more needs to be done to protect our food supply? If yes, what are some steps that could be taken? If not, why not?

3. Why are some farm animals, such as dairy cows, given added hormones? Do you think those hormones pose a risk to humans? Why or why not?

B With your classmates, talk about the ways each of the following poses a danger to our food supply.

1. air pollution
2. antibiotics in farm animals
3. global warming
4. industrial chemicals
5. overpopulation
6. pesticides

Key Vocabulary

As you read "Hormones in Food: Should You Worry?", pay attention to the following words and phrases and see if you can work out their meanings from the contexts.

injections	wind up
artificially	reassure
hormones	excess
regulates	contributing
approve	stringent

Hormones in Food: Should You Worry?

The following article was published in the Huffington Post[1], *Jan. 31, 2011.*

1   A salmon that grows to market size twice as fast as normal. Dairy cows that produce 15 percent more milk. Beef cows that grow 20 percent faster.

2   What do these hyper-productive animals have in common? Thanks to **injections** and implants (in the case of cows) or genetic engineering (in the case of salmon), they contain **artificially** high levels of sex or growth **hormones**.

3   Are these hormones dangerous to the humans who eat the food or drink the milk? The food industry says no—and the Food and Drug Administration[2] (FDA) agrees, at least when it comes to cows.

4   The FDA, which **regulates** the use of hormones in livestock, hasn't yet decided whether it will **approve** the sale of a genetically engineered salmon patented by the

---

1 *Huffington Post* 《赫芬顿邮报》
2 Food and Drug Administration （美国）食品与药物管理局

Bluefin tuna are farmed and fattened off the coast of Spain for the restaurant sushi market.

biotech company AquaBounty[3]. If the salmon—which is wired to produce growth hormone year-round, instead of just in the spring and summer—gets an OK from the agency, it will be the first genetically engineered animal to **wind up** on your dinner plate. (Genetically engineered fruits and vegetables have been around for years.)

5   The FDA's stamp of approval isn't likely to **reassure** those who worry that **excess** hormones in the food supply are **contributing** to cancer, early puberty in girls, and other health problems in humans. For years, consumer advocates and public health experts have fought to limit the use of hormones in cows, and some support a ban on the practice similar to the one in place in Europe, where food regulations are generally more **stringent** than in the U.S.

6   But it is not clear if such hormones truly are bad for our health. Surprisingly little research has been done on the health effects of these hormones in humans, in part because it's difficult to separate the effects of added hormones from the mixture of natural hormones, proteins, and other components found in milk and meat. Buying organic may reassure shoppers, but there's little proof these products are safer.

---

3 AquaBounty 水恩科技公司

Vocabulary

A What are the meanings of the **bold** words or phrases? Circle the letter of the best answer.

1. Thanks to **injections**, they contain high levels of growth hormones.
   a. placing something inside by cutting it open
   b. administering a substance by mouth
   c. placing a substance on the skin
   d. putting liquid into something with a special needle

2. They contain **artificially** high levels of growth hormones.
   a. not by man
   b. by nature
   c. by accident
   d. not naturally

3. The FDA regulates the use of **hormones** in livestock.
   a. artificial substances that people take to be healthier
   b. substances in the body that affect growth and development
   c. natural substances that carry oxygen in the blood stream
   d. liquids in the body that control body temperature

4. The FDA **regulates** the use of hormones in livestock.
   a. makes exceptions for
   b. controls by rules
   c. refuses to allow the use of
   d. gets in the way of

5. The FDA hasn't decided whether it will **approve** the sale.
   a. act upon
   b. bring into use
   c. let go of
   d. agree to

6. It will be the first genetically engineered animal to **wind up** on your dinner plate.
   a. disappear
   b. take aim
   c. end up
   d. move

7. The FDA's stamp of approval isn't likely to **reassure** those who worry.
   a. make free from fear
   b. cause doubt in
   c. provide an explanation for
   d. cause anxiety to

8. FDA approval isn't likely to reassure those who worry that **excess** hormones in the food supply are contributing to cancer.
   a. more than usual
   b. lesser in quality
   c. unacceptable
   d. unwanted

9. FDA approval isn't likely to reassure those who worry that excess hormones in the food supply are **contributing to** cancer.
   a. becoming the main cause of
   b. helping to bring about
   c. interfering with
   d. removing the possibility of

10. In Europe, food regulations are generally more **stringent** than in the U.S.
    a. changeable
    b. important

c. severe   d. complicated

B Answer these questions with complete sentences.

1. What might **reassure** you that you'll like a certain movie?
   _____

2. What product do you use that is **artificially** made?
   _____

3. What happens when you do an **excess** of exercise?
   _____

4. What is a **stringent** rule in most schools?
   _____

5. How does the government **regulate** the speed of cars on a roadway?
   _____

C Now write your own sentences. Use the following words or phrases in the sentences: **hormones**, **contributing**, **injections**, **wind up**, and **approve**.

_____
_____
_____

Reading Comprehension

A Circle the letter of the best answer.

1. Which of the following statements is the main idea of the reading?

   a. Salmon and cows contain artificially high levels of growth hormones.

   b. Fruits and vegetables that are genetically engineered will be the food on our dinner plates.

   c. All hyper-productive animals have something in common and no one knows clearly about its safety.

   d. Research about high levels of hormones in foods should be done to reassure people.

2. Who have been fighting for the limited use of hormones in cows?

   a. The majority of consumers.

   b. Consumer advocates and FDA.

   c. The government and food industries.

   d. Consumer advocates and public health experts.

3. Why has research hardly been done on the health effects of added hormones in humans?

   a. Partly because research may be too costly and there is no financial support from governments.

   b. Partly because such research is too hard to tell the effects of hormones added by people from those of the natural ingredients in milk and meat.

Unit 6 Nutrition   147

c. Partly because not many people have such health awareness about artificial hormones in foods.

d. Partly because there is little proof that organic food is safer than food with added hormones.

4. What can be inferred from the first two paragraphs?

   a. Animals injected with hormones take less time to reach maturity.

   b. Salmon is popular with consumers since it grows very fast.

   c. Hormones don't necessarily help milk production.

   d. The animals that are hyper-productive have lots of things in common.

5. What can we infer according to the sentence "some support a ban on the practice similar to the one in place in Europe" in Paragraph 5?

   a. There are lots of consumer advocates and public health experts in Europe.

   b. Milk in France does not have added hormones.

   c. Regulations on the use of hormones in France are as stringent as in the U.S.

   d. There is currently a severe abuse of added hormones in Europe.

B Find information in the reading to answer these questions. Note the number of the paragraph where you find the answer. Discuss your answers with a partner.

1. Why does a genetically engineered salmon from AquaBounty grow faster than a normal one?

   _____
   _____

   Paragraph: _____

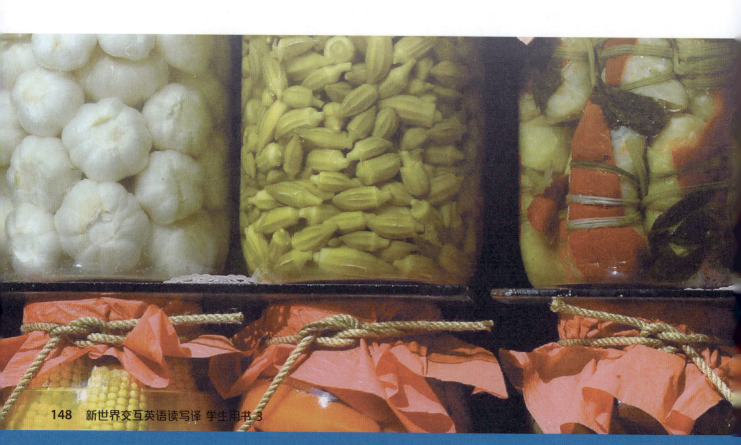

2. Why can't the FDA's stamp of approval give reassurance to consumers about the food with hormones?

   _____
   _____

   Paragraph: _____

3. What will happen if the Food and Drug Administration approves the sale of a salmon patented by the biotech company?

   _____
   _____

   Paragraph: _____

Critical Thinking

Discuss these questions with your classmates.

1. What is the purpose behind the genetic engineering of our food sources?
2. What are some of the pros and cons of genetically engineered foods?
3. What are some potential problems that might occur as a result of the introduction of genetically modified plants and animals on our farms and fish farms?
4. What problems related to our food supply do you think we'll face in the future?
5. What can we do now to ensure the availability and safety of our future food supply?

Writing

Writing Skills

The Cause-and-Effect Essay

A popular type of essay is the *cause-and-effect essay*. This form is frequently used in academic writing. In college, your history teacher may ask you to write about the causes of the American Civil War; your biology teacher may ask you to write on the three effects of a snake bite; your sociology teacher may ask you to explain the high number of people living to over 100 in Japan.

- There are three types of cause-and-effect essays.
    1. The **cause analysis essay** explains causes.
    2. The **effect analysis essay** explains effects.
    3. The **causal chain essay** explains causes that lead to effects in a chain.

Cause Analysis Essay

- Very few situations can be traced back to a single cause. Something usually has several causes or a combination of causes that lead to an effect. For example, consider this question: *Why do some children have a low IQ?* For some, it may be a result of early malnutrition, which slows brain growth; for others, it may be a result of exposure to toxins, such as lead, which damage the nervous system. It may be caused by the lack of a stimulating environment. It may also be caused by parents who do not encourage their children or spend time with them. If you examined the topic further, you might find that family size could also be a cause.

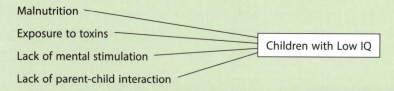

- In the cause analysis essay, the **thesis statement** should state the causes to be discussed.

    EXAMPLE: Low IQ in children is generally caused by the following factors: malnutrition in childhood, lack of a stimulating environment, and lack of interaction with their parents.

- Each **body paragraph** should discuss one of the causes mentioned in the thesis statement.

- The **conclusion** should restate the thesis and provide a general comment on the topic.

Effect Analysis Essay

- Just as there can be many causes for something, a cause can have several effects. For example, many people consume caffeine in one form or another, which has the effect of making them alert. However, addiction to caffeine can have many negative effects such as restlessness, insomnia, heartbeat irregularities, and even high blood pressure, which may lead to other serious problems.

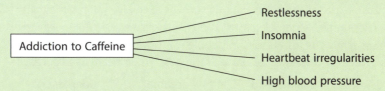

- In Reading 1, the effects of food additives are explained. Notice that reference is made to the cause before explaining the effect. It is important to understand which is the cause and which is the effect. Look at the following examples:

  Cause: The additives sodium nitrite and sodium nitrate are two closely related chemicals that have been used for centuries to preserve meat.
  Effect: Nitrite has been considered an important cause of stomach cancer in the United States, Japan, and other countries.

  Cause: The sugar substitute aspartame is sold commercially as Equal® or NutraSweet® and is used in many diet beverages.
  Effect: About 1 out of 20,000 babies cannot metabolize 1 of the 2 substances that aspartame is made from, and toxic levels of that substance can result in mental retardation.
  Effect: Some people who have consumed aspartame have reported dizziness, headaches, and even seizures.
  Effect: Aspartame may be linked to an increased risk of brain tumors.

- The **thesis statement** of an effect analysis essay should state the effects to be discussed.

  EXAMPLE: Eating fast food regularly may cause our bodies to be deficient in vitamins and minerals we need to maintain good health; also, eating fast food can be very addictive, and people accustomed to it rarely change their eating habits.

- As for the effect analysis essay, select two or three major effects to write about, and in each **body paragraph** write about one of those effects. In the thesis statement above, two effects have been selected. Therefore, the first body paragraph will explain the effect of eating fast food on health, and the second body paragraph will explain the addictive effect of eating fast food regularly. Support each effect with relevant examples and/or facts.

- The **conclusion** should restate the thesis and provide a general comment on the topic.

Causal Chain Essay

- In the causal chain type of cause-and-effect essay, one cause leads to an effect, which leads to another cause, and so on, creating a chain of causes and effects.

    cause → effect → cause → effect

- For example, bad weather conditions such as excessive rainfall may affect farmers' vegetable crops, causing the vegetable crops to die. This makes vegetables scarce, causing prices to rise in the supermarkets. This results in people not buying very many vegetables, because they are so expensive. Since people eat fewer vegetables, their health is affected.

    excessive rainfall → damage to vegetable crops → vegetable prices go up → people eat fewer vegetables → people become less healthy

- The **thesis statement** of a causal chain essay should state the three or four steps in the chain.

    EXAMPLE: The use of the artificial hormone BST to increase milk production indirectly affects human health, since the cows that are given BST get infections and are treated with antibiotics, which then get into our milk supply.

- It is important to break the chain into three or four major steps. Each **body paragraph** should describe one step in the chain stated in the thesis statement. Each step should be supported with details.

- The **conclusion** should restate the main points in the chain and provide a comment on the topic.

Exercise 1

Identify which is the Cause (C) and which is the Effect (E) in each set of sentences.

1. _____ Accident death rates dropped by 30 percent.

    _____ A seat belt law was passed.

    _____ Motorists were required to wear seat belts.

2. _____ Carla burned 500 calories per week.

    _____ Carla's blood pressure was lower.

    _____ Carla exercised 45 minutes each day.

3. _____ Social and work-related pressures have increased in modern times.

    _____ People are more at risk for stress-related illnesses, such as heart attacks.

4. _____ The sun's ultraviolet rays penetrate the deeper layer of the skin.

    _____ Skin cancer is one of the most common forms of cancer in the United States.

    _____ The protective ozone layer in the atmosphere is decreased by pollutants.

5. _____ Most American women over the age of 50 consume half of their daily calcium requirements.

    _____ Calcium in bones is gradually depleted, leaving them weak and brittle—a condition called osteoporosis.

_____ In this country, older women suffer approximately 5 million fractures each year.

6. _____ People who walk daily have healthier cardiovascular systems.

_____ Aerobic exercises allow the heart and lungs to utilize oxygen more efficiently.

7. _____ Flu viruses are highly contagious and are spread through close contact with infected persons.

_____ Flu epidemics spread rapidly through the workplace.

8. _____ Antibiotics have been overprescribed by doctors for decades.

_____ Over a period of time, bacteria can become resistant to antibiotics when repeatedly exposed to them.

_____ A medical crisis exists because many antibiotics are no longer useful for combating diseases.

Exercise 2

In each sentence of the paragraph, underline the cause once and the effect twice.

1. Ear pain occurs when there is a buildup of fluid and pressure in the middle ear. Often during a cold or an allergy attack, particularly in small children, the ear tube becomes swollen shut, preventing the normal flow of fluid from the middle ear. Fluid begins to accumulate, causing stuffiness and decreased hearing. Sometimes a bacterial infection starts in the fluid, resulting in pain and fever. Ear pain and ear stuffiness can also result from high altitudes, such as when flying in an airplane or driving in the mountains. Swallowing will frequently relieve the pressure in the ear tube.

2. Eating candy can produce acids in the body. Consuming carbohydrates can even produce an alcoholic condition in your body. One of our great orators, William Jennings Bryan, gave speeches nationwide about the bad effects of drinking alcohol, causing more than one person to change his drinking habits. Ironically, Bryan himself died of an alcoholic stomach as a result of eating 13 pancakes with syrup for breakfast. Eating the pancakes, which are full of carbohydrates, and the sugary syrup created a kind of alcoholic brew in his stomach. This innocently consumed brew produced alcohol poisoning, which in turn led to his death.

Exercise 3

The most frequent use of the causal chain essay is in the sciences—for example, in essays about biological or weather cycles. Plan the causal chain for one of the following topics.

1. The cutting of forests in the Amazon
2. The killing of elephants for ivory
3. The global use of non-degradable plastic products

Writing Practice

Write an Essay

Choose one of the following topics to write a cause-and-effect essay.

1. An effect analysis on eating junk food regularly
2. The causes or effects of pollution
3. The causes or effects of the use of pesticides

Pre-Write

A Use one of the pre-writing techniques you prefer (see Unit 2), and find three causes or three effects.

B Find an article that contains information on your topic and write a brief summary of it (see Unit 4). Find a short excerpt from the article that you would like to include in your essay and paraphrase it (see Unit 3). Find one or two statements written by the author that you might like to quote in your essay (see Unit 5).

C Work on a thesis statement for your essay.

Organize Your Ideas

A Write your thesis statement. Include the three causes or effects.

B Order your causes or effects.

C Provide supporting ideas and details for each cause or effect.

D Make a detailed outline.

Write a Rough Draft

Using your detailed outline and any notes you made in Pre-Write, write a rough draft of your essay.

Revise Your Rough Draft

Check the thesis statement, unity, development, coherence and purpose of your rough draft.

Edit Your Essay

Work with a partner or your teacher to edit your essay. Check the spelling, punctuation, vocabulary, and grammar.

Write Your Final Copy

After you edit your essay, you can write your final copy.

Translation

A Translate the following passage into English.

食品添加剂是一些添加在食物里的化学物质，它们能让食品保持新鲜，增强食品的色彩、增加食品的味道或口感。它们大致包括食物色素、调味剂或者各种防腐剂。有些人会对个别食物添加剂很敏感，但这并不意味着人们需要对所有含有添加剂的食物持怀疑态度。事实上，那些含有化学物质和食品添加剂的食物的安全程度并不总亚于那些含有天然化学物质的食品，比如谷氨酸钠（MSG）在乳酪和西红柿里的天然含量远比食品里添加的含量高，而且它们并没有什么危害性。

B Translate the following passage into Chinese.

If your child has attention deficit hyperactivity disorder (ADHD), it's not because he or she played too many video games, spent long hours watching TV, or ate the wrong kinds of foods. In fact, researchers think the cause of ADHD is largely genetic. But it is tempting to look for dietary factors that could be making symptoms worse. In particular, a possible link between ADHD and certain foods—including food dyes and preservatives—has been suspected since the 1970s. Still, despite decades of research, experts can't agree on whether eliminating dye-containing foods from a child's diet can ease ADHD symptoms like hyperactivity and impulsivity. Although it is possible that a very small group of children who are allergic to artificial colorings or preservatives may show improvement in symptoms on restriction diets, evidence is insufficient to recommend widespread use of restriction diets to treat a child's ADHD symptoms.

Weaving It Together

Unit Project

Conduct a survey among your classmates. Give a presentation of your survey results to your classmates. You may ask the following questions:

1. What is the consequence of eating junk food regularly?
2. What are the causes or effects of pollution?
3. What are the causes or effects of the use of pesticides?
4. As consumers, what responsibilities and awareness should we have to maintain our health?

Searching the Internet

A Search the Internet for information about three artificial sugar substitutes. Find answers to these questions:

1. What trade names do they go by?
2. In which countries are they used and how long for?
3. In which countries are they banned?

B Search the Internet for information about one of the following cause or effect topics. Share the information with your classmates.

Causes of anorexia	Effects of caffeine
Causes of obesity	Effects of lead poisoning
Causes of diabetes	Effects of vitamin supplements

C You may use your research later to write a cause-and-effect essay.

What Do You Think Now?

Refer to the very beginning of this unit. Do you know the answers now? Complete the sentence, or circle the best answer.

1. Artificial sweeteners (are/are not) dangerous for our health.
2. The average American (eats/does not eat) about five pounds of food additives per year.
3. People worry about the safety of _____ foods.
4. (Not much/A lot of) research has been done on the health effects of hormones in our food.

Broadening Your Horizon

A

Why the FDA Has Never Looked at Some of the Additives in Our Food

Advocacy groups say they're concerned that Americans are consuming foods with added flavors, preservatives and other ingredients that have never been reviewed by regulators for immediate dangers or long-term health effects.

B

Food Fights

Get ready for another wave of anti-GMO mania. This one is about to begin with the news that genetically modified salmon are about to be approved by the U.S. Food and Drug Administration (FDA).

C

Chipotle Says Adios to GMOs, as Food Industry Strips Away Ingredients

Chipotle's announcement that it has removed all GMOs from the items on its menu is part of a growing food industry trend. From left: Nestle chocolates, Chipotle tortillas, Diet Pepsi, Kraft Macaroni & Cheese Dinner, a Subway sandwich. All of these companies have dropped ingredients over the past year in response to consumer demands.

UNIT 7
Issues for Debate

A great white shark is lured up to cages so that tourists can take dramatic photos in South Africa.

WHAT DO YOU THINK?

Answer these questions with your best guess. Circle *Yes* or *No*.

1. Are lions protected from hunters in Africa? Yes   No
2. Is hunting regulated in the United States? Yes   No
3. Did an American write the first ™book on animal rights? Yes   No
4. Does Germany give rights to animals in its constitution? Yes   No

Reading ▪ 1

Pre-Reading

Preparing for the Reading Topic

A Discuss these questions with your classmates.

1. Is the hunting of wild animals popular in China? Why or why not?

2. Do you think there is any reason to hunt animals in the 21st century? Why or why not?

3. Should some African animals be protected from hunters? If yes, which should be protected? If not, why not?

B Identify which of the following animals are on the endangered species list. Place an *X* in front of them. Then match each animal with the country or region in which it is usually found. Place the letter of the country after the animal.

_____ 1. black rhino   _____ a. China

_____ 2. giraffe   _____ b. Brazil

_____ 3. giant tortoise   _____ c. Kenya

_____ 4. Bengal tiger   _____ d. Galapagos Islands

_____ 5. giant panda   _____ e. Zimbabwe

_____ 6. jaguar   _____ f. India

Key Vocabulary

As you read "Tweet Touches Off Heated Debate", pay attention to the following words and see if you can work out their meanings from the contexts.

outraged	species
condemn	eliminating
opponents	irrelevant
funds	indefensible
dubious	enforce

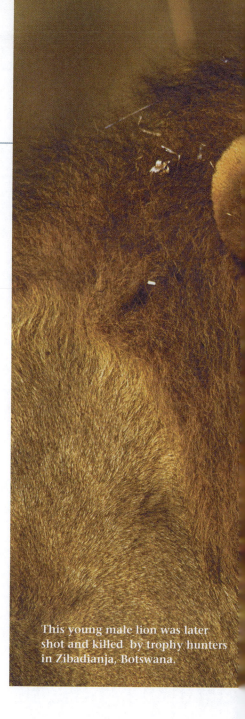

This young male lion was later shot and killed by trophy hunters in Zibadianja, Botswana.

Tweet Touches Off Heated Debate

The following article is by Brian Clark Howard[1], National Geographic Magazine, Nov. 19, 2013.

1 For Melissa Bachman[2], a tweet may be worth a thousand insults.

2 The Minnesota[3]-based big game hunter and Outdoor Channel TV personality has stirred up controversy by posting a picture to Twitter[4] of herself and a dead lion. Bachman tweeted, "An incredible day hunting in South Africa! Stalked inside

---

1 Brian Clark Howard 布瑞恩·克拉克·霍华德，国家地理杂志撰稿人
2 Melissa Bachman 梅丽莎·巴赫曼，美国某电视狩猎节目女主持人
3 Minnesota 明尼苏达州，美国州名，首府为圣保罗
4 Twitter 推特，美国一家提供社交和微博服务的网站平台

60-yards on this beautiful male lion... what a hunt!"

3   Many **outraged** people have taken to social media to **condemn** the picture, often with harsh words for Bachman. To be sure, others have defended Bachman's right to hunt, pointing out that controlled lion hunting is legal in South Africa (safari[5] hunting was recently outlawed in Botswana[6]).

4   But that didn't stop **opponents** of lion hunting from launching a petition on Change.org[7], asking the government of South Africa to deny future entry to Bachman, whom it says is "an absolute contradiction to the culture of conservation." That petition has more than 300,000 signatures so far.

RESPONDING TO CRITICISM

5   The group that facilitated Bachman's hunt, Maroi Conservancy[8], is a private preserve of 21,000 acres (8,500 hectares) along the Limpopo River[9] in South Africa. Established in 1993, the preserve offers safari hunts of various animals.

6   In response to criticism over Bachman's photo, the Maroi Conservancy posted a note on its Facebook[10] page saying, "Our motto is 'conservation through sustainable hunting'." The conservancy said meat from animals shot on site is distributed to the local community. **Funds** raised through hunting are used to shore up[11] fences and guard against poachers, the note added.

7   The conservancy wrote that it had recently hosted Bachman, who had expressed her desire to shoot a lion. "There are no lions on Maroi as they do not occur here naturally," the group noted.

8   So the Maroi Conservancy arranged for Bachman to work with another hunting outfitter in Zeerust[12], in North West Province[13]. "We did not benefit financially from this hunt," the group argued.

9   Bachman received the necessary government permits, and "the lion was not drugged or enclosed in a camp. It was free roaming on more than 2,000 hectares (4,900 acres). Melissa is a professional hunter and in no way is she involved in **dubious** practices," they wrote.

10 The group said that it will not apologize for facilitating the hunt, and added, "As for all the negative commentary towards us, please consider how much you have contributed to conservation in the past years. If you are not a game farmer and struggling with dying starving animals, poaching and no fences in place to protect your animals and crop, please refrain from making negative derogatory comments." The conservancy claims there are more animals in South Africa now than 100 years ago,

---

5 safari 游猎；（在非洲观看野生动物的）旅行
6 Botswana 博茨瓦纳，非洲南部邻南非的一个内陆国，首府为哈博罗内
7 Change.org 一家成立于2007年的社会公益请愿网站
8 Maroi Conservancy 马瑞欧（私营）保护区
9 Limpopo River 林波波河，非洲东南部的一条大河，林波波在当地语言中意为"鳄"，因此又称鳄鱼河
10 Facebook 脸书，一家社交网络服务网站
11 shore up 支撑住以修缮（围栏等）
12 Zeerust 济勒斯特，南非共和国的一个城镇
13 North West Province 西北省，南非共和国九省之一

thanks in part to money raised through regulated hunting.

THE HEATED HUNTING DEBATE

11   Bachman's story touches on a controversy that has been brewing across Africa and beyond. Those who support limited hunting of big cats argue that money raised through fees and expeditions can be invaluable in conservation efforts. In the other camp, people argue that every lion is precious and should be protected, even if the **species** has not been officially declared endangered (there are thought to be 32,000 to 35,000 lions living in 27 African countries, and the U.S. Fish and Wildlife Service[14] has spent recent months debating whether to upgrade the animal's status).

12   *National Geographic News* recently featured a pair of essays that looked at both sides of this debate. Melissa Simpson, director of science-based wildlife conservation for the Safari Club International Foundation[15], wrote in September that wildlife officials need money more than anything else in order to save lions from their biggest threat, poaching. That money can be best supplied by controlled hunts, each of which can provide up to $125,000, Simpson argued.

13   She pointed to the example of Tanzania[16], which generated $75 million through lion hunting from 2008 to 2011. Simpson wrote that although non-hunting photo safaris also have contributed to conservation efforts in Tanzania, 11 out of 15 wilderness areas could continue to operate only after being subsidized by hunting revenue.

14   "As with the regulated hunters in the United States, the regulated hunters in Africa make a vital contribution to conservation efforts, primarily through the revenues their hunting expeditions generate for local communities and wildlife resource agencies," Simpson wrote.

15   Jeff Flocken[17], North American director for International Fund for Animal Welfare[18], wrote in July that lion hunts "are unsustainable and put more pressure on the species". Flocken noted that about 600 lions are killed by "safari" or "trophy" hunters a year. About 60 percent of those animals are killed by Americans, he added.

16   Flocken noted that trophy hunters tend to be most interested in killing big males, which he said could impact evolution of the species by **eliminating** some of the healthiest genes.

17   When a dominant male is killed, it can also lead to more deaths, Flocken wrote. Other males in the area may fight to the death to overtake the pride. The winner then may assassinate any cubs sired by[19] the previous leader.

BREEDING MALE?

18   When it comes to Bachman's picture, media reports suggest that she had indeed shot a male in his prime. National Geographic reached out to Bachman for comment but has not heard back. We also sent the picture to a big cat conservation biologist, who asked not to be named because of the sensitivity of this story.

---

14 U.S. Fish and Wildlife Service 美国鱼类和野生动物服务组织
15 Safari Club International Foundation 游猎俱乐部国际基金会
16 Tanzania 坦桑尼亚，国家名，位于非洲东部，首都为多多马
17 Jeff Flocken 杰夫·付罗肯，动物福利国际基金会北美区主管
18 International Fund for Animal Welfare 动物福利国际基金会
19 sired by 是……的后代

19   Our source confirmed that the lion in the photo looks to be of breeding age, but added that the question is really **irrelevant**. "All lion hunting in South Africa is done on private reserves," they said. "Just because you can't see the fence doesn't mean it's not a canned hunt[20]. It's a completely artificial industry, where these animals are bred, sold, then released in paddocks[21] to be shot."

20   The lion was most certainly not a breeding member of a wild population, so its death should not directly affect the status of the species, our source added. "On an organismal[22] level, shooting a lion is **indefensible**," they said. "But on a conservation level, it's a double-edged sword. There simply is not enough money for conservation, but there is a lot of interest in hunting."

21   Taking aim at hunters, Luke Hunter[23], vice president of big cat conservation group Panthera, wrote in March, "The entire process that allows hunting big cats in Africa needs a complete overhaul to purge its excesses and **enforce** far stricter limits on which lions can be hunted and how many. That would force hunters to produce the conservation benefits of which they constantly boast but only rarely produce."

Vocabulary

Vocabulary in Context

A What are the meanings of the **bold** words? Circle the letter of the best answer.

1. Many people were **outraged** when they saw the photo of Bachman with a dead lion.
   a. motivated
   b. furious
   c. unhappy
   d. saddened

2. "Many outraged people have taken to social media to **condemn** the picture…"
   a. disapprove
   b. remove
   c. confront
   d. damage

3. "But that didn't stop **opponents** of lion hunting from launching a petition…"
   a. people who are against
   b. people who feel sorry for
   c. people who agree with
   d. people who don't believe in

4. "Melissa is a professional hunter and in no way is she involved in **dubious** practices," they wrote.
   a. known as against the law or morality
   b. thought to be completely out of the ordinary
   c. unclear as to the quality or correctness of
   d. stated to be the approved action

5. The conservancy said the **funds** from hunting were used against poachers.
   a. surplus
   b. money

---

20 canned hunt 动物被圈禁在一定区域或围栏内的狩猎
21 paddock 围场
22 organismal 生物的，有机体的
23 Luke Hunter 卢克·亨特，大型猫科动物保护组织Panthera副主管

164 新世界交互英语读写译 学生用书 3

      c. fame   **d.** bad name

6. "...people argue that every lion is precious and should be protected, even if the **species** has not been officially declared endangered..."

    a. a grouping composed of several types of plants or animals

    b. a category that includes all plants or animals

    c. a class of animal that includes several sub-types

    d. a group of animals or plants of the same kind

7. "...which he said could impact evolution of the species by **eliminating** some of the healthiest genes."

    a. changing   **b.** increasing

    c. removing   **d.** decreasing

8. "Our source confirmed that the lion in the photo looks to be of breeding age, but added that the question is really **irrelevant**."

    a. related   **b.** the same

    c. a necessary part   **d.** not connected

9. "On an organismal level, shooting a lion is **indefensible**," they said.

    a. cannot be understood   **b.** cannot be repeated

    c. cannot be saved   **d.** cannot be excused

10. "The entire process... needs a complete overhaul to purge its excesses and **enforce** far stricter limits on which lions can be hunted..."

    a. cause to be carried out   **b.** create a new form of

    c. loosen the restrictions on   **d.** change the rules about

B Answer these questions with complete sentences.

1. What benefit might you get by **eliminating** some of your possessions?

2. What recent piece of news has **outraged** people?

3. Where do most people keep their **funds**?

4. What bird **species** do you like?

5. What behavior might a parent **condemn**?

C Now write your own sentences. Use the following words in the sentences: *irrelevant*, *enforce*, *opponents*, *indefensible*, and *dubious*.

Unit 7 Issues for Debate   **165**

Vocabulary Building

A Read the list of verbs below. Find the verbs in the reading that have the same meaning. The paragraph in which the verbs appear is given in parentheses. Note that the verbs in the reading may be in a different tense. The first one is done for you.

1. refuse   _____deny_____ (Paragraph 4)
2. defend   _____ (Paragraph 11)
3. highlighted   _____ (Paragraph 12)
4. make   _____ (Paragraph 13)
5. have a direct effect   _____ (Paragraph 16)
6. eliminate   _____ (Paragraph 21)

B Complete these sentences with the correct form of the verbs you found in Exercise A.

1. People who _____ limited hunting of big cats say that it raises money for conservation.
2. Many people wanted the government of South Africa to _____ Bachman entry to the country.
3. Essays looking at both sides of the hunting debate were _____ in *National Geographic News*.
4. Trophy hunters like to kill male lions, and this may _____ the species.
5. In Africa, hunting expeditions _____ money for wildlife agencies.
6. Luke Hunter said that the way big cats are hunted needs to be changed to _____ the lack of controls.

Reading Comprehension

A Circle the letter of the best answer.

1. The main idea of the reading is that _____.
   a. the Maroi Conservancy defends its support of Bachman's hunt
   b. Bachman's hunt shows how hunting can generate money for conservation
   c. hunts like Bachman's demonstrate the need for enforcement of limits on lion hunting
   d. there are opinions on both sides of a debate on the benefits of hunting big cats

2. Paragraphs 18–21 (Breeding Male?) are mainly concerned with _____.
   a. whether the lion in Bachman's picture was a breeding male
   b. the need to address the problems concerning hunting big cats
   c. how hunting on private reserves is really "canned" hunting
   d. the necessity for stricter limits on which lions can be hunted

3. Which of the following cannot be a defense for Bachman's hunt?
   a. Controlled lion hunting is legal in South Africa.
   b. Bachman received the necessary government permits.

c. Maroi Conservancy facilitated the hunt.

   d. Conservation efforts may benefit from the money raised by the hunt.

4. Which can be inferred from the reading?

   a. Bachman no longer hunts lions in Africa.

   b. The Maroi Conservancy is more interested in conservation than promotion.

   c. Jeff Flocken thinks that some lion hunting should be allowed.

   d. The Maroi Conservancy finds people do not understand the situation that game farmers are faced with.

5. Which of the following is in contradiction with Melissa Simpson's statements?

   a. Controlled hunts can provide lots of money for conservation.

   b. In Tanzania more attention is given to the photo safaris.

   c. The biggest threat facing the lions is poaching.

   d. Many wildness areas cannot operate without hunting revenue.

B Complete the summary below using the list of words in the box.

defended	supplied	eliminate	petition	stirred
condemned	fund	enforced	response	permits
protect	contradiction	alter	conflict	regulate

Melissa Bachman, a TV host as well as a hardcore game hunter, is at the center of an international firestorm after posting a picture of herself and a dead lion to Twitter. The proud kill photo she posted **1.** _____ up controversy. While many outraged animal rights activists **2.** _____ the hunting some supporters **3.** _____ the hunter's right. Many South Africans have started a **4.** _____ to have Bachman banned from their country and regard her as an absolute **5.** _____ to the culture of conservation. Maroi Conservancy, a private reserve which had facilitated Bachman's hunt, posted a note on its Facebook page as a **6.** _____ to the criticism. They argued that Bachman received the government's **7.** _____ and it was not an enclosed or canned hunt. Melissa Simpson claimed that wildlife officials needed money more than anything else in order to save lions from poaching and the money could be best **8.** _____ by controlled hunts. Jeff Flocken noted that lion hunts were unsustainable and trophy hunt could **9.** _____ some healthiest genes. Luke Hunter, the vice president of Panthera, pointed out that much stricter limits on lion hunting should be **10.** _____ and the entire process that allowed big cats hunting in Africa needed a complete overhaul.

Critical Thinking

Discuss these questions with your classmates.

1. On which side of the debate do you find yourself? Do you sympathize with Melissa Bachman and other hunters like her? Or are you on the side of the outraged people who responded on social media? Explain your stand on this topic.

2. In "canned" hunts, captive-bred, often hand-reared lions are confined in enclosed spaces on private hunting reserves, guaranteeing marksmen easy trophy heads in exchange for fees. What is your opinion on "canned" hunts? Should they be allowed? Why or why not? What did the source mean when he or she said "It's a completely artificial industry"?

3. What are the benefits to society of conservation efforts in general? Do you envision wilderness areas in existence 100 years from now? How do you see the reciprocal relationships between the tourism industry and the preservation?

4. In July 2016, a woman was mauled by a tiger and another dragged to death after they got out of their car during the family's visit to a wildlife park in Beijing. Many netizens criticized the women who got out of the car first; what is your opinion on this tiger-attack incident?

5. Nowadays considerable efforts and funds are spent on the conservation of wild animals especially some privileged ones like the giant panda; many people complain that they are not treated so decently as a panda. What is your opinion on this?

Reading 2

Pre-Reading

Preparing for the Reading Topic

A Discuss these questions with your classmates.

1. How do animals help humans?
2. Are all animals the same, or are some more important than others?
3. Do you agree with society's treatment of animals?

B Match the animals with the ethical treatment issue concerning them.

_____ 1. elephants   a. laboratory experiments
_____ 2. cats   b. crowded water enclosures
_____ 3. chickens   c. entertainment
_____ 4. chimpanzees   d. feed lots
_____ 5. bulls   e. chaining
_____ 6. fish   f. small wire cages
_____ 7. cattle   g. declawing
_____ 8. dogs   h. cruel sports

Key Vocabulary

As you read "Do Animals Have Rights?", pay attention to the following words and phrases and see if you can work out their meanings from the contexts.

endowed with	deliberately
pursuit of	humanely
prevailed	resemble
issue	consciousness
abuse	restrictions on

Unit 7 Issues for Debate   169

Do Animals Have Rights?

Donkeys carry loads of hay down a road in rural Ethiopia.

1   The American Declaration of Independence said "all men are created equal, that they are **endowed... with** certain unalienable Rights, that among these are Life, Liberty and the **pursuit of** Happiness." This was one of the first statements of human rights. Back in 1776, this was a new idea, but today we are used to the idea that as humans we have certain basic rights.

2   Our right to equal treatment also means that we have to treat other people as equals. In the beginning, equal rights and responsibilities were limited to certain groups. Over time, justice **prevailed**, and with the civil rights movement came the modern belief that it is not acceptable to discriminate on the grounds of sex, race, or religion.

3   Does the belief in equality, freedom, and the right to be treated in a certain way apply to animals as well? Do animals also have "certain unalienable Rights" among which are "Life, Liberty and the pursuit of Happiness"? This **issue** is at the heart of the

debate about animal rights.

4 Animal welfare societies started in Britain and the United States in the early 1800s. In fact, the United Kingdom passed laws to protect animals from **abuse** before there were any laws to protect children. The Royal Society for the Prevention of Cruelty to Animals[1] (RSPCA) was founded in 1824 to find and punish people who **deliberately** harmed animals. The first book on animal rights was written by an Englishman, Henry Salt[2], in 1892. His book and the animal rights movement that he started were based on two ideas: that human beings are not made to eat meat and that we have a moral duty to treat animals "like us". This means we should behave toward animals just as we behave toward other human beings. Not everybody supported Salt's ideas, but he made people think about animals and their rights.

5 In 1948, human rights became universal with the United Nations Declaration of Human Rights[3], which stated that "recognition of the inherent dignity and of the equal and inalienable rights of all members of the human family is the foundation of freedom, justice and peace in the world." But it is only since the 1970s that the idea of animals having rights just as humans do has developed. It started with an essay written by Peter Singer[4] in which he used the term *animal liberation*. In his article in the *New York Review of Books*, Singer wrote about how animals should be treated, and this started the debate that continues up to now.

6 How similar are animals to humans? Can some animals feel and think in ways similar to humans? Scientists have discovered that chimpanzees have many similarities with humans. Researchers who work with chimpanzees say they experience almost every emotion we do. They use tools, think ahead, and take care of one another. At Central Washington University[5] in the United States, a chimpanzee named Washoe[6] learned American Sign Language; she used it to communicate with humans and even taught it to another chimpanzee called Loulis. Researchers also claim that other creatures, such as gorillas, whales, and dolphins, are more like us than we think. On May 20, 2003, the BBC reported on a study published in the U.S. journal *Proceedings of the National*

---

1 The Royal Society for the Prevention of Cruelty to Animals （英国）皇家防止虐待动物协会
2 Henry Salt 亨利·萨尔特（1851–1939），英国作家和社会改革活动家，倡导动物权利，著有《动物权利与社会进步的关系》
3 the United Nations Declaration of Human Rights 联合国《世界人权宣言》
4 Peter Singer 彼得·辛格，澳大利亚伦理学家，动物保护运动的倡导者，著有《动物解放》
5 Central Washington University 中央华盛顿大学，公立综合性大学，位于华盛顿州的爱伦斯堡
6 Washoe 沃肖（1965—2007），一只学会美国手语的黑猩猩，以内华达州沃肖县对其命名

Academy of Sciences[7], which claims, "Chimpanzees are so closely related to humans that they should properly be considered as members of the human family, according to new genetic research. Scientists from the Wayne State University[8], School of Medicine, Detroit[9], U.S.A., examined key genes in humans and several ape species and found our 'life code' to be 99.4 % the same as chimps."

7   A British animal welfare group called Compassion in World Farming[10] (CIWF) started campaigning in the 1980s to win a new status in law for animals. They wanted animals to be given the status of "sentient beings[11]" (i.e., possessing a level of conscious awareness and able to have feelings). After years of petitions, the concept that animals are sentient was finally recognized by the European Union[12] (EU) in 1997. A statement was added to the EU treaty that required that their welfare, as sentient beings, be properly taken into account in the development of the Community's policies on agriculture, transport, the internal market, and research. Compassion in World Farming accepts that farm animals will be killed for their meat, but argues that they should be treated **humanely**. As reported by the BBC on May 9, 2003, the group believes that animals that live in communities "often exhibit signs of morality that **resemble** human behavior. There is evidence that some animals do have some level of morality and some concern over other animals. Living within a group requires a moral code of behavior. Zoologists who have spent their professional lives studying animal behavior, either by observation or by experiments to test their mental capacities, believe that many animals feel and think." Joyce D'Silva[13], chief executive of CIWF, told BBC News Online, "This has huge implications for all the ways we use animals and implies that all farm animals are entitled to humane lives and deaths." If it is true that some creatures have a capacity for **consciousness** similar to that of human beings, then there is justification for giving them rights like those of humans.

8   Germany has become the first European nation to vote to guarantee animal rights in its constitution. Before the vote, animals in Germany were already protected by laws governing the conditions under which they could be held in captivity. The issue of animal rights had been debated among German politicians for years. Then, in 2002, lawmakers in Germany voted to add "and animals" to a clause that obliges the state to respect and protect the dignity of humans. With this new law, there will be tighter **restrictions on** the use of animals for testing cosmetics and nonprescription drugs. Lawmakers in Germany said that they would give more funding to projects that look at alternatives to using animals for experiments.

9   Today, animal welfare groups around the world continue with their work to change laws to protect animals and make their existence more humane.

---

7 *Proceedings of the National Academy of Sciences* 《美国国家科学院院刊》
8 Wayne State University 韦恩州立大学，美国著名公立研究型大学，位于密歇根州的底特律市
9 Detroit 底特律，美国密歇根州的最大城市，被称为汽车之城
10 Compassion in World Farming 世界农场动物福利协会
11 sentient being 佛教中指具有意识和情感的众生
12 European Union 欧盟，1993年11月《马斯特里赫特条约》正式生效，欧盟正式成立
13 Joyce D'Silva 乔伊斯·德席尔瓦，世界农场动物福利协会首席主管

Vocabulary

A What are the meanings of the **bold** words or phrases? Circle the letter of the best answer.

1. All men are **endowed with** certain unalienable rights.
   - a. intelligent enough to have
   - b. gifted with
   - c. capable of
   - d. lacking in

2. All men have the right to "Life, Liberty and the **pursuit of** Happiness".
   - a. search for
   - b. judgment of
   - c. answer to
   - d. decision for

3. Over time, justice **prevailed**.
   - a. failed
   - b. succeeded
   - c. existed
   - d. lived

4. This **issue** is at the heart of the debate about animal rights.
   - a. answer
   - b. doubt
   - c. danger
   - d. question

5. The United Kingdom passed laws to protect animals from **abuse**.
   - a. anger
   - b. attack
   - c. mistreatment
   - d. worry

6. The Royal Society for the Prevention of Cruelty to Animals (RSPCA) was founded to punish people who **deliberately** harmed animals.
   - a. intentionally
   - b. forcefully
   - c. accidentally
   - d. strongly

7. Compassion in World Farming (CIWF) argues that animals should be treated **humanely**.
   - a. politely
   - b. cruelly
   - c. caringly
   - d. generously

8. The group (CIWF) believes that animals that live in communities "often exhibit signs of morality that **resemble** human behavior".
   - a. are exactly like
   - b. are a new form of
   - c. are separate from
   - d. are similar to

9. Chimpanzees have a richly developed **consciousness**.
   - a. knowledge
   - b. awareness
   - c. memory
   - d. order

10. With this new law, there will be tighter **restrictions on** the use of animals for testing.
    - a. limitations on
    - b. methods for
    - c. areas for
    - d. systems for

B Answer these questions with complete sentences.

1. What current **issue** do you have strong feelings about?

2. In what public places might there be **restrictions on** the use of cell phones?

3. What is very helpful to someone's **pursuit of** success?

4. Why might someone **deliberately** miss an appointment?

5. Whom do you **resemble** in your family?

C Now write your own sentences. Use the following words or phrases in the sentences: *consciousness*, *humanely*, *endowed with*, *prevailed*, and *abuse*.

Reading Comprehension

A Circle the letter of the best answer.

1. This reading is mainly about _____.
   a. human rights
   b. animal rights
   c. the laws for human rights protection
   d. the laws for animal rights protection

2. Paragraph 6 is mainly about the fact that _____.
   a. chimpanzees experience almost every emotion humans do
   b. chimpanzees can use sign language to communicate with humans
   c. there are many similarities between humans and animals
   d. chimpanzees are members of the human family

3. It can be inferred from the reading that _____.
   a. animals are treated more humanely now in the EU than in the past
   b. in Germany animals are respected like humans
   c. Henry Salt's philosophy is accepted by most Europeans
   d. many people don't think animals are conscious

4. Which of the following statements is not true?
   a. CIWF does not accept that farm animals should be killed for meat.
   b. Some animals show concern about others.
   c. Both human rights and animal rights used to be neglected.
   d. Some animals are more like us than we think.

5. Which of the following statements is not true about Germany?

   a. The use of animals for testing is restricted.

   b. As for animal rights, there is no debate among the politicians now.

   c. Animal rights have been guaranteed by its constitution.

   d. The respect and protection of human dignity are written in the law.

B Find information in the reading to answer these questions. Note the number of the paragraph where you find the answer. Discuss your answers with a partner.

1. Who wrote the first book on animal rights? What does this book want to express?
   _____
   _____

   Paragraph: _____

2. Who is Washoe? How is Washoe related to the topic of the reading?
   _____
   _____

   Paragraph: _____

3. What is CIWF? What are its claims?
   _____
   _____

   Paragraph: _____

Critical Thinking

Discuss these questions with your classmates.

1. How would you respond if you saw an animal being treated badly? Do you think that people who deliberately harm animals should be punished? Do you think people have gone too far, or not far enough to protect the rights of animals? Why?

2. What are some farming practices that are considered inhumane to animals? In what ways could farm animals be treated more humanely?

3. Does it make sense to treat animals humanely and then eat them? Why or why not? Do you think humans will ever stop eating meat?

4. Some claim that the zoo animals are not supposed to be in captivity for man's benefit and should be freed. What is your opinion on this issue?

5. Do you think animals have human characteristics? In what ways are animals and humans commonly compared? Do you agree with Henry Salt that we have a moral duty to treat animals like us?

6. Some linguists claim that human languages denote the human-centered beliefs in the vocabulary and even grammar. What is your opinion on this statement?

Writing

Writing Skills

The Argument Essay

In an *argument essay*, just like an oral argument, you must win the person over to your way of thinking. You must appeal to the other person's sense of reason by being logical and by providing evidence.

- Assume that the reader does not agree with you. If the reader did agree, then you would not have to write an argument. When arguing your point, remember not to insult the reader in any way just because his or her opinion may be different from yours. Insulting your reader with a statement such as "People who believe that handguns should not be banned are all killers" will weaken your argument. Always be respectful and logical.

- Just presenting your own reasons is not sufficient to convince the reader. To convince the reader, you must understand your opponents' position and the reasons they would give to support their opinion. It is, therefore, essential to know both sides of the argument in order to make a strong case for your position.

- In an argument essay, it is important to support your opinion with pertinent facts and statistics coming from reliable authority.

The Introduction

- Introduce the topic by giving background information. It is important that the reader understand the issue to be argued. Define any terms that are unclear. If you were going to argue against animal testing, you would have to define animal testing very clearly before taking your stand.

- The *thesis statement* in an argument essay is different from those in other types of essays. In the argument essay thesis, you have to be persuasive and take a stand or choose a side on an issue.

The Body Paragraphs

- The body paragraphs give reasons for your opinion and support them with evidence or facts. Each body paragraph relates to a point of the argument stated in your thesis. The body paragraphs should be ordered so that the strongest reason is last.

- A characteristic of the argument essay is that it recognizes the opposing view and proves it wrong, or *refutes* it. This means that you start with one of your opponents' viewpoints and use your superior reasons to prove that it is wrong. Generally, the refutation occurs in the last body paragraph.

- The following is an example argument and refutation.

    Argument
    Using animals for testing is wrong and should be banned. Animals feel pain in the same way as humans. Causing pain to an animal is the same as causing pain to a human being. If animals have the same right to be free from pain, we should not experiment on them.

Each year in the United States, about 70 million animals are used in research. They are tortured, injured, and killed in the name of science by private companies, government agencies, and educational institutions. Animals are used to test the degree of harmfulness of certain household products and their ingredients. Sometimes animals are injected with infectious diseases such as AIDS. In most cases, the animals are left to die with no certainty that this suffering and death will save a single life or benefit humans in any way at all. There is no reason to make innocent animals suffer; other alternatives should be used.

Refutation
While it is true that many animals suffer and die in scientific research, it is a fact that we need animal research for advances in medicine and product safety. Most of today's medical advances, such as vaccines, surgical procedures, and so on, would not have been possible without animal experimentation. Computer models or artificial substances cannot work in the same way as blood, bones, or organs can in a living system. It is not possible to predict the course of many diseases or the effects of treatments without testing them on living systems. At present, scientists do not know enough about living systems to replicate one on a computer. Until that day comes, animals are vital in research if medical progress is to continue.

The Conclusion

- In the conclusion, summarize the main points of your argument or restate the thesis. End your conclusion with a strong statement, such as a demand for action or an alternative solution.

Outline for an Argument Essay

- The following is a brief example outline for an argument essay.

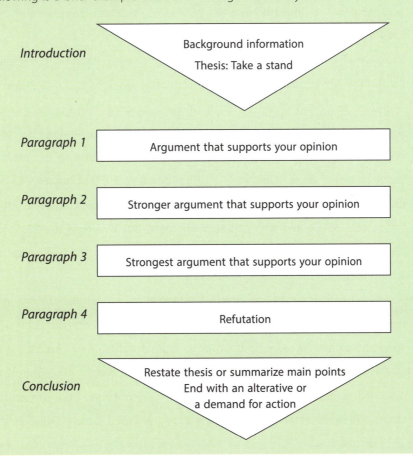

Exercise

Read the following argument essay written by a student. Then answer the questions at the end of the essay.

Against Animal Rights

There has been a debate about animal rights for a long time. People who support animal rights believe that animals should have the same rights as humans, such as the right to equality and freedom. It is important that as rational humans we protect all living things in order to keep our planet in balance. However, it is my belief that this does not mean that animals should have the same rights as humans. First, animals are not the same as humans; they are different. If we give them the same rights as humans, we will not be able to eat meat or keep animals for pleasure and entertainment, which humans have done since the beginning of time.

Are animals like us? This is a complex problem. It is true that animals feel pain like humans, but they cannot think like humans. Animals cannot reason. Animals do not survive by making conscious decisions. Human rights are about conscious decisions we make about how we live and how we behave toward one another. Can animals make decisions like that? Animals cannot tell you what their rights are. No animal can take you to court for violating its rights. This does not mean we should treat them cruelly or in a way that is not humane. On the contrary, we should treat them with respect because they are different from us. We need to treat all living species with respect to keep our planet in balance.

Secondly, if animals had the same rights as humans, then people who killed animals for food would be murderers. Anyone who ate a steak or had turkey for Thanksgiving would go to prison. What would happen if someone killed a fly? Most people who support animal rights are vegetarians. They believe that humans are supposed to be vegetarians, and that their teeth and stomachs are designed to eat vegetables and not meat. However, there is historical and biological proof that humans have always eaten meat. They hunted animals for food and ate seeds and nuts. Humans are not different today. Not only could we no longer eat meat, but we could not wear leather or fur. Humans have been wearing the skins of animals since the beginning. If it was not wrong then, why should it be wrong now?

My opponents say it is wrong for people to use animals in experiments or use them for entertainment. The Web page of PETA (People for the Ethical Treatment of Animals), an organization that supports animal rights, says, "Animals are not ours to eat, wear, experiment on or use for entertainment." People who support animal rights have such strong beliefs about this that they have set fire to or destroyed fur and leather stores and medical laboratories. They have even used violence to show their beliefs. Is

this humane toward other humans? They believe that animals should not be used for research even if it would lead to cures for deadly diseases. Using animals for research has saved and will save human lives, but this does not matter to animal rights supporters. Is it better to experiment on humans rather than animals? They think so. They also believe that animals should not be used for entertainment. This means that we could not have zoos to go to, and we could not even have pets because to have pets would be a form of pleasure and entertainment.

In conclusion, I think people want to protect all species to keep the earth in balance. Some want to give animals the same rights as humans, while others, which I think are the majority, want to give animals the right to be free from cruelty and torture. Even if some animals are more conscious of the world than others, this does not mean animals are "like us". They are different and cannot have the same rights as humans. If they did, we could no longer eat meat, wear their skins, or use them for research. This does not mean we should be cruel to animals. We should respect them and treat them humanely.

1. Underline the thesis statement.
2. Is the writer's argument for animal rights or against them? State his or her three reasons.
3. Are the three reasons developed in the body paragraphs?
4. Examine the first paragraph. Do all the ideas support the writer's opinion?
5. Are the main points restated in the conclusion? Does the writer give a final comment on the topic?

Writing Practice

Write an Essay

Choose one of the following topics to write an argument essay.

1. Using animals for medical research
2. Using animals for entertainment
3. Raising fish in enclosed water pens (fish farms)
4. Raising animals in large numbers for food (factory farming)

Pre-Write

A Use one of the pre-writing techniques you prefer (see Unit 2), and find three reasons for and three reasons against some aspect of the topic.

B Find an article that contains information on your topic and write a brief summary of it (see Unit 4). Find a short excerpt from the article that you would like to include in your essay and paraphrase it (see Unit 3). Find one or two statements written by the author that you might like to quote in your essay (see Unit 5).

C Work on a thesis statement for your essay.

Organize Your Ideas

A Write your thesis statement. Include the three reasons for or against some aspect of the topic.

B Order your reasons. Choose the opponents' arguments that you will refute.

C Decide what kinds of support would be relevant. Go to the library or use the Internet to get relevant facts.

D Make a detailed outline.

Write a Rough Draft

Using your detailed outline and any notes you made in Pre-Write, write a rough draft of your essay.

Revise Your Rough Draft

Check the thesis statement, unity, development, coherence and purpose of your rough draft.

Edit Your Essay

Work with a partner or your teacher to edit your essay. Check the spelling, punctuation, vocabulary, and grammar.

Write Your Final Copy

After you edit your essay, you can write your final copy.

Translation

A Translate the following passage into English.

由于中国大熊猫的数量显著增加，这一萌物的官方地位已经从"濒危"下降到了"易危"。国际自然保护联盟（IUCN）红色名单更新的时候，宣布了此项变化。中国视熊猫为国宝，在中国的努力之下，其数量从濒临灭绝的边缘恢复了过来。最新估计，成年大熊猫的数量已经达到了1864只。国际自然保护联盟更新后的报告说道："大熊猫的地位从濒危下降到了易危，这说明中国政府保护大熊猫的努力是卓有成效的。"

B Translate the following passage into Chinese.

Leading experts are working on a revision to a national regulation on the management of laboratory animals, which, if adopted, is expected to greatly improve the management and protection of the animals. A draft of the new rules includes changes to the Regulation on the Management of Laboratory Animals, which was adopted in 1988, according to Sun Deming, chairman of the Welfare and Ethics Committee of the Chinese Association for Laboratory Animal Sciences, also known as CALAS, who is helping to formulate the new rules. The Regulation on the Management of Laboratory Animals, a major guideline on the management of animals used in scientific testing, has been revised several times since it was enacted. It is primarily intended to ensure that animals used in laboratory experiments are of sufficiently high quality, in terms of health, to meet the demands of scientific research. The regulation also includes a number of articles related to the animals' welfare, such as stipulations that the scientists conducting the experiments must "take good care of the animals and do not provoke or abuse them".

Weaving It Together

Unit Project

Collect the information of a certain animal or some kind of birds. Then give a presentation to your classmates and share the information with them. The presentation can be related to the following topics:

1. Do you think of the animals or birds as sentient beings? Why or why not?
2. Can they communicate with you? If yes, how?
3. Do you like them? Why or why not?
4. How do you feel about keeping wild animals captive in zoos?

Searching the Internet

A Search the Internet for information about similarities of humans to one of the following: gorillas, chimpanzees, or dolphins. Find answers to these questions:

1. How much do our genes resemble theirs?
2. How are their senses similar to ours?
3. What behaviors do they have that are similar to ours?

B Search the Internet for information about trophy hunting in Africa. Share the information with your classmates.

C You may use your research later to write an argument essay.

What Do You Think Now?

Refer to the very beginning of this unit. Do you know the answers now? Complete the sentence, or circle the best answer.

1. Lions (are/are not) protected from hunters in Africa.
2. Hunting (is/is not) regulated in the United States.
3. _____ wrote the first book on animal rights.
4. _____ gives rights to animals in its constitution.

Broadening Your Horizon

Trophy Lion Hunts Unsustainable

Trophy or "sport" hunting can be used as a conservation measure, with the money that hunters pay being used to help protect a wider population of animals. But are trophy lion hunts sustainable?

B

Opinion: Killing of Marius the Giraffe Exposes Myths About Zoos

Zoos, most of us think, are meant to be safe havens for animals, places where they are loved and protected. Zoos tell us that they are educational places, too, where we can watch and learn about creatures we might otherwise never have a chance to see. But this passage tells another story.

C

Watch Villagers Save Drowning Leopard in Dramatic Rescue

After a big team effort, animal rescue experts and villagers saved a leopard from drowning in a large open well in India.

UNIT 8
Readings from Literature

Interior of the nine-story, ultra-modern, Stuttgart City Library, Germany, which opened in November 2011

WHAT DO YOU THINK?

Answer these questions with your best guess. Circle *Yes* or *No*.

1. Does a first-person narrator know what all the characters are doing in a story?   Yes   No
2. Are all stories written from the same point of view?   Yes   No
3. Does the title of a poem help us to understand its meaning?   Yes   No
4. Is the theme of a poem the same as the subject?   Yes   No

Reading 1

Pre-Reading

Preparing for the Reading Topic

A Discuss these questions with your classmates.

1. What is a horror story?
2. Do you like horror stories and movies? Why or why not?
3. What types of characters do we find in horror stories?

B Work with a partner. Write or tell each other about a horror story using the following words and phrases.

beating heart	midnight
full moon	shrieking owl
graveyard	skeleton

Key Vocabulary

As you read "The Tell-Tale Heart", pay attention to the following words and see if you can work out their meanings from the contexts.

senses	chilled
insulted	stain
pale	scream
slipped	investigate
terror	agony

The Tell-Tale Heart

The following is an adaptation of The Tell-Tale Heart *by Edgar Allan Poe[1].*

1   True! Nervous—very nervous I had been and I am! But why do you think I am mad? The disease has sharpened my **senses**—not destroyed them, especially my sense of hearing. I heard all things in heaven and in the earth. I heard many things in hell. How could I be mad? Listen how calmly I can tell you the whole story.

2   It is impossible to say how the idea first entered my mind. I loved the old man. He had never wronged me. He had never **insulted** me. I had no desire for his gold. I think it was his eye! Yes, his eye. He had the eye of a bird, a vulture—a **pale** blue eye, with a film over it. Every time the eye looked at me, my blood ran cold; and so—very slowly—I made up my mind to take the old man's life and free myself of the eye forever.

3   You think I am mad. Madmen do not know anything. But you should have seen me. You should have seen how cleverly and carefully I worked.

4   I was very kind to the old man during the whole week before I killed him. And every night, about midnight, I opened the door of his room—oh, so very gently! And then when I made an opening big enough for my head, I put in a dark lantern, it was closed so no light came out. Then I put in my head, slowly, very slowly, so I would not disturb the old man's sleep. When my head was well in the room, I opened the lantern just enough to let a single, thin ray of light fall on the vulture eye. I did this for seven nights, but found that the eye was always closed, so it was impossible to do the work. It was not the old man that was a problem for me, but his Evil Eye.

5   On the eighth night, I was more careful than usual. I opened the door and put my head in and was about to open the lantern when my finger **slipped** on a piece of metal and made a noise. The old man sat up in bed, and cried out, "Who's there?"

---

1 Edgar Allan Poe 埃德加·爱伦·坡（1809—1849），美国诗人、评论家和短篇小说家

6   I kept still and said nothing. For a whole hour I did not move. During that time, I did not hear him lie down. He was still sitting up in bed, listening—just as I have done, night after night. Then I heard a noise, and knew it was the sound of human **terror**. It was the low sound that comes from the bottom of the soul. I knew that sound well. Many a night, when it was late and the world slept, it came up from deep within my chest. I knew what the old man felt and felt sorry for him. But I laughed to myself because I knew he had been lying awake since the first noise when he turned in bed. His fears had been growing all this time.

7   When I had waited a long time, I decided to open the lantern a little, very little. You cannot imagine how very carefully I did it. Finally, a single ray of light came out of the lantern and fell upon the vulture eye.

8   It was open-wide, wide open and I grew angry as I looked at it. I saw it clearly—a pale blue eye with a horrible film over it that **chilled** my bones. I could not see anything else of the old man's face or person because I had directed the light exactly on the spot.

9   Then I could hear a low, dull, quick sound such as a watch makes when inside a piece of cotton. I knew that sound well, too. It was the beating of the old man's heart. My anger grew more.

10 I kept still. I hardly breathed. I held the lantern without moving it and tried to keep the ray of light upon the eye. But the beating of the heart increased. It grew quicker and quicker and louder and louder every second. The old man's terror must have been extreme! The beating grew louder and louder every moment!

11 Now at the dead hour of the night, in the horrible silence of the house, this strange noise excited me to uncontrollable terror. For some minutes I stood still. But the beating grew louder, louder!

12 I was afraid. I thought the neighbors would hear the sound! The old man's hour had come! With a loud shout, I opened the lantern and jumped into the room. He screamed once—only once. I quickly threw him to the floor and pulled the heavy bed over him. Then I smiled at myself at what I had done. The heart went on beating for many minutes but that did not bother me.

13 After a while it stopped. The old man was dead. I removed the bed and examined the body. I put my hand over his heart and held it there for a few minutes. There was no movement. He was dead. His eye would not trouble me anymore.

14 If you still think I am mad, you will change your mind when you listen to the careful steps I took to hide the body. I worked quickly but in silence. I took up three pieces of wood from the floor and placed his body under the room. I put the boards back so well that no human eye, not even his could have seen anything wrong. There was nothing to wash out—no **stain** of any kind—no blood whatsoever. I had been too careful for that.

15 By the time I had finished, it was four o'clock in the morning. As the clock sounded the hour, there was a knock at the front door. I went down to open it with a light heart. What did I have to fear? Three police officers entered. A **scream** had been heard during the night by a neighbor, and the police officers had come to **investigate**.

16   I smiled because I had nothing to fear. I told them that the scream was mine. I had screamed in my dream. I said the old man was away. I took my visitors all over the house. I told them to search well and search everywhere. Then I took them to his room. I brought chairs there and told them to sit and rest. I put my own chair exactly over the spot under which the dead body lay.

17   The officers believed me. I was completely at ease and happily answered their questions. But after a while I felt weak and wished that they would go away. My head ached and I heard a ringing in my ears. But the officers continued to sit and chat. The ringing was getting clearer. I talked more freely to get rid of the feeling. But it continued. Soon I realized that the noise was not in my ears.

18   I spoke more loudly but the sound increased. What could I do? It was a low, dull, quick sound like that of a watch inside a piece of cotton. I could hardly breathe and yet the officers did not hear it. I talked more quickly but the sound grew even louder. Why wouldn't they go away? I walked across the room angrily but the noise grew louder. Oh God! What could I do? I swung the chair on which I had been sitting and scraped it on the floor, but the noise grew louder and louder. The men continued to chat happily. Was it possible that they did not hear the noise?

19   Oh God! They heard! They knew! They were making fun of me and of my horror. That is what I thought, that is what I think. But anything was better than this **agony**. I couldn't stand seeing their happy faces. I felt that I must scream or die! And the noise was louder, louder, louder!

20   "Stop pretending," I screamed, "I admit it! I killed the man! Look under the floorboards! Here! Here! It is the beating of his ugly heart!"

Vocabulary

Vocabulary in Context

A What are the meanings of the **bold** words or phrases? Circle the letter of the best answer.

1. "The disease has sharpened my **senses**—not destroyed them…"
   a. emotions, such as sadness and happiness
   b. natural abilities, such as seeing and tasting
   c. the brain's ability to store information
   d. the strength of the body's muscles and sinews

2. "He had never **insulted** me."
   a. said something that caused hurt feelings
   b. caused bodily harm to
   c. was unfair to or caused difficulty for
   d. stopped from doing something

3. "He had the eye of a bird, a vulture—a **pale** blue eye…"
   a. lesser amount of color
   b. deeper shade of color
   c. more brilliant color
   d. mixture of different colors

4. "… my finger **slipped on** a piece of metal and made a noise."
   a. got stuck on
   b. slid out of place on
   c. struck a blow against
   d. touched lightly

5. "Then I heard a noise, and knew it was the sound of human **terror**."

    a. much excitement   **b.** deep sorrow

    c. strong hatred   **d.** great fear

6. "... a pale blue eye with a horrible film over it that **chilled** my bones."

    a. caused to feel pain   **b.** made extremely hot

    c. prevented from moving   **d.** caused to become cold

7. "There was nothing to wash out—no **stain** of any kind..."

    a. torn section that wasn't mended   **b.** broken part that wasn't fixed

    c. dark spot that wasn't there before   **d.** extra layer that was added

8. "A **scream** had been heard during the night by a neighbor..."

    a. sound like laughter   **b.** low sound showing sadness

    c. angry shout   **d.** loud sound expressing fear or pain

9. "... the police officers had come to **investigate**."

    a. inquire about the reasons for something   **b.** offer help in time of need

    c. seize someone who has committed a crime   **d.** take someone to a safe place

10. "But anything was better than this **agony**."

    a. doubt or uncertainty   **b.** strong feeling of pity

    c. great pain or suffering   **d.** overwhelming feeling of guilt

B Answer these questions with complete sentences.

1. What have you ever **slipped** on?

2. When have you felt **terror**?

3. What might cause a person to **scream**?

4. What do you like to eat that is **chilled**?

5. Why might a person suddenly turn **pale**?

C Now write your own sentences. Use the following words in the sentences: ***investigate***, ***agony***, ***stain***, ***insulted***, and ***senses***.

Vocabulary Building

A Match the words in the reading that go together to make common phrases. The first one is done for you.

- _c_ 1. beating   a. my mind
- ___ 2. sitting up   b. my bones
- ___ 3. disturb   c. of the heart
- ___ 4. laughed   d. the old man's sleep
- ___ 5. made up   e. in bed
- ___ 6. chilled   f. to myself

B Complete these sentences with the words you found in Exercise A.

1. I put my head through the door very slowly because I didn't want to _____.
2. When I saw the horrible blue eye with a film over it, it _____.
3. I _____ to kill the old man and never again see the eye.
4. I heard a low, quick sound like that of a watch. It was the _____ of the old man.
5. For a whole hour, the old man was _____ and listening.
6. I _____ because I knew the old man had been sitting up in bed since he heard the first noise.

Reading Comprehension

A Circle the letter of the best answer.

1. The narrator is telling the story because he _____.
   - a. wants everyone to think he's a madman
   - b. believes he didn't kill the old man
   - c. wants to show that he's not insane
   - d. wants to admit his crime

2. The narrator wanted to kill the old man because he _____.
   - a. always hated the old man
   - b. wanted to inherit the old man fortune
   - c. was afraid of the old man's eye
   - d. enjoyed frightening the old man

3. What did the narrator do with the old man's body?
   - a. He hid the body under the chair.
   - b. He pulled the body under the bed.
   - c. He hid the body under the floorboards in the bedroom.
   - d. He just threw the body to the floor.

4. The officers weren't leaving because _____.
   - a. they were enjoying their visit
   - b. the narrator was behaving strangely
   - c. they knew a murder had occurred
   - d. they could hear the heart beating

5. The beating heart the narrator hears is most likely _____.

   a. the old man's heart

   b. a watch in his pocket

   c. his own heart

   d. a sound outside the house

B Complete the summary below using the list of words in the box.

beneath	sanity	presence	stand	absence
morality	sneaks	investigate	madness	waking
However	observe	cautiously	sensation	freezes

Before the narrator tells his story, he claims that he is nervous but not mad, and offers his calmness in the narration as proof of his **1.** _____. He then explains how he cannot **2.** _____ the sight of the vulture eye, although he has no resentment for the man. Every night around midnight, in the week before the murder, the narrator **3.** _____ into the old man's room and **4.** _____ shines a lantern onto the man's eye. **5.** _____, because the eye is always closed, he doesn't kill him. On the eighth night, while opening the door, the narrator accidentally touches a piece of metal and makes a noise, **6.** _____ the old man. The narrator **7.** _____, but even after an hour, the old man does not return to sleep. It seems that he feels afraid and senses someone's **8.** _____. Finally, the narrator decides to open the lantern slightly. A ray of light falls on the offending eye that is wide open, which inflames our protagonist and drives him to murder. When the police come to **9.** _____, he is so confident that he brings them into the murdered man's room for the investigation and seats himself directly above the floorboards **10.** _____ which the murdered man lies. All goes well until he begins to "hear" a ringing, which grows louder and louder and becomes unbearable to him. Terrified by the violent beating of the heart and convinced that the officers are aware of not only the heartbeat, but his guilt as well, the narrator breaks down and confesses his crime.

Critical Thinking

Discuss these questions with your classmates.

1. What effect does fear have on our lives? When is being afraid a good thing? When is being afraid detrimental to us?

2. Why are horror stories and movies so popular? Why do people love to be frightened?

3. How powerful is guilt? What effect does it have on our behavior? Is a sense of guilt greater in some people than in others? Why, or why not?

4. Criminologists try to determine why people commit crimes. What are the reasons for people to commit crimes?

5. What are the reasons for the murderer in Poe's story to commit his crime? Analyze and explain your answers.

Reading 2

Pre-Reading

Preparing for the Reading Topic

A Discuss these questions with your classmates.

1. What are some virtues or qualities considered morally good or desirable in a person?
2. How do parents teach these virtues to their children?
3. What are three virtues that your parents taught you?

B Match each virtue on the left with an action on the right.

_____ 1. dependability
_____ 2. patience
_____ 3. forgiveness
_____ 4. humility
_____ 5. perseverance
_____ 6. kindness

a. Even though you win the game, you don't boast about it to your friends.

b. You help an older person up a flight of stairs.

c. You say no to an invitation for coffee because every afternoon you work at the bookstore.

d. You accept your friend's apology for forgetting your birthday.

e. You calmly wait while the salesperson takes care of other customers.

f. You don't quit your math class even though you're struggling to get a passing grade.

Key Vocabulary

As you read "If", pay attention to the following words and phrases and see if you can work out their meanings from the contexts.

blaming	trap
make allowance	worn-out
deal	heap
give way	loss
triumph	hold on

If

by Rudyard Kipling[1]

1 Rudyard Kipling 鲁德亚德·吉卜林（1865—1936），英国小说家和诗人

1   If you can keep your head when all about you
    Are losing theirs and **blaming** it on you,
    If you can trust yourself when all men doubt you,
    But **make allowance** for their doubting too;
    If you can wait and not be tired by waiting,
    Or, being lied about, don't **deal** in lies,
    Or being hated don't **give way** to hating,
    And yet don't look too good, nor talk too wise:

2   If you can dream—and not make dreams your master;
    If you can think—and not make thoughts your aim;
    If you can meet with **Triumph** and Disaster
    And treat those two impostors just the same;
    If you can bear to hear the truth you've spoken
    Twisted by knaves[1] to make a **trap** for fools,
    Or watch the things you gave your life to, broken,
    And stoop and build 'em up with **worn-out** tools:

3   If you can make one **heap** of all your winnings
    And risk it on one turn of pitch-and-toss,
    And lose, and start again at your beginnings,
    And never breathe a word about your **loss**;
    If you can force your heart and nerve and sinew[2]
    To serve your turn long after they are gone,
    And so **hold on** when there is nothing in you
    Except the Will which says to them: "Hold on!"

4   If you can talk with crowds and keep your virtue,
     Or walk with Kings—nor lose the common touch,
    If neither foes nor loving friends can hurt you,
    If all men count with you, but none too much;
    If you can fill the unforgiving minute
    With sixty seconds' worth of distance run,
    Yours is the Earth and everything that's in it,
    And—which is more—you'll be a Man, my son!

---

1 knave（古英语）不诚实、不能信赖的人
2 sinew 肌腱

Vocabulary

A What are the meanings of the **bold** words or phrases? Circle the letter of the best answer.

1. "Are losing theirs and **blaming** it on you..."
   a. saying someone is the cause for something bad
   b. giving someone something they need
   c. thanking someone for doing good
   d. being sorry for something that happened to someone

2. "But **make allowance** for their doubting too..."
   a. accept someone's statements as the truth
   b. see things as they really are
   c. forgive others for their actions
   d. consider someone else's opinions or abilities

3. "Or, being lied about, don't **deal in** lies..."
   a. stay away from   b. make excuses for   c. delight in   d. be a part of

4. "Or being hated don't **give way to** hating..."
   a. fight off   b. protect   c. yield to   d. join with

5. "If you can meet with **Triumph** and Disaster..."
   a. tragedy   b. adventure   c. success   d. difficulty

6. "Twisted by knaves to make a **trap** for fools..."
   a. plan for deceiving or tricking a person
   b. way to help someone get out of trouble
   c. way to force someone to do something
   d. foolish course of action

7. "And stoop and build 'em up with **worn-out** tools..."
   a. newly made and strong
   b. almost ruined from use
   c. slightly used
   d. unsuitable for a certain use

8. "If you can make one **heap** of all your winnings..."
   a. things separated into small groups
   b. things in a pile on top of each other
   c. things neatly placed in a row
   d. things thrown in every direction

9. "And never breathe a word about your **loss**..."
   a. a person's sad state of affairs
   b. something a person possesses
   c. something a person no longer has
   d. something a person desires

10. "And so **hold on** when there is nothing in you..."
    a. take possession of something
    b. let go of things one can no longer have
    c. stop a course of action for a time
    d. continue in spite of difficulties

B Answer these questions with complete sentences.

1. What is one **triumph** you have had in your life?

2. What might a boss **make allowance** for when training a new employee?

3. What do you sometimes put in a **heap**?

4. What **loss** have you experienced?

5. What is something you keep using but is **worn-out**?

C Now write your own sentences. Use the following words or phrases in the sentences: **hold on**, **blaming**, **give way**, **deal**, and **trap**.

Reading Comprehension

A Read the poem again to understand its meaning. Circle the letter of the best answer.

1. "If you can keep your head when all about you

   Are losing theirs and blaming it on you,"

   a. Don't blame others for the things that happened to you.

   b. Act according to your beliefs even if it makes you unpopular.

   c. Follow the lead of others who can show you the way.

   d. Keep fighting even after others have given up.

2. "If you can trust yourself when all men doubt you,

   But make allowance for their doubting too;"

   a. Only trust for yourself and no one else.

   b. Be self-confident but consider opposing ideas.

   c. Don't doubt others because then you are doubting yourself.

   d. Give people a reason to believe in you.

3. "Or watch the things you gave your life to, broken,

   And stoop and build 'em up with worn-out tools:"

   a. Pick yourself up and start again when things go wrong.

   b. Be willing to do something different from what you've always done.

   c. Don't have regrets about the past.

   d. Always be ready to fix things when they break.

4. "If you can force your heart and nerve and sinew

   To serve your turn long after they are gone,

   And so hold on when there is nothing in you

   Except the Will which says to them: 'Hold on!'"

a. Serve others before you serve yourself.

   b. Work hard for the good of other people.

   c. Let go of dreams you know you can never have.

   d. Never give up even when you think you can't go on.

5. "If you can fill the unforgiving minute

   With sixty seconds' worth of distance run,"

   a. Learn to forgive others.

   b. Keep at what you're doing and never stop.

   c. Make good use of your time.

   d. Allow yourself some time to relax in life.

B Find information in the poem to answer these questions. Note the number of the stanza where you find the answer. Discuss your answers with a partner.

1. How does the narrator look upon success and failure?

   _____
   _____

   Stanza: _____

2. What is the narrator's attitude toward those who would twist a person's truths into lies?

   _____
   _____

   Stanza: _____

3. If a person has the good fortune to be among the rich and powerful, what does the narrator expect of that person?

   _____
   _____

   Stanza: _____

Critical Thinking

Discuss these questions with your classmates.

1. What virtues or principles do you try to live by? Why is it difficult to live according to these principles?

2. Do you think it is harder to have principles or virtues today than in the past? Why or why not?

3. What character traits and virtues are Chinese people known for? Explain your answers.

4. Do you think different cultures live by different virtues? Are there certain principles that are shared over all societies? Explain your answers.

5. Do you think the virtues mentioned in this poem are as applicable to women as they are to men? Why or why not?

Writing

Writing Skills

Narrator and Point of View

Usually, when we ask someone what his or her point of view is, we are asking about the person's opinion. When we are discussing literature, however, *point of view* means the perspective of the person who is telling the story. The story can be presented through the eyes of a character or through the eyes of the author, or the point of view can alternate between characters or between the author and characters. The author can choose from some of the following options.

- **First-Person Narrator.** "The Tell-Tale Heart" is told in the first person. This means that we know only what is going on in the mind of the narrator. We know only about events that he sees or experiences. We don't know what the old man thinks, though we can guess by trying to interpret his actions and words. The first-person point of view can be used to increase suspense, because some information can be hidden from readers and then used to surprise them later. It can also create empathy as we try to identify and understand the narrator's feelings. On the other hand, we may come to dislike or distrust the narrator, and in this case we may notice a gap between what the narrator says and what the author wants us to think. This is called *irony*, a figure of speech, and Poe uses it extensively in his storytelling.

- **Third-Person Narrator.** A story told in the third person refers to all characters as "she", "he", or "they", not as "I". But here there is also a choice for the writer. The author can write as an "omniscient", or all-knowing, third-person narrator who sees everything. In this case, the author is not restricted as to time or location and can see everything that goes on in all the characters' minds. Or the author can write from a limited third-person point of view. In this case, the story is limited to the thoughts of a major character, and nothing is described in the story unless it is seen, felt, or experienced by this character.

- In the examples below, the same excerpt is told by a first-person narrator, a limited third-person narrator, and an omniscient third-person narrator.

    EXAMPLE 1 **First Person:**
    The bright sunlight hurt my eyes as we emerged from the dark theater. I was still shivering from the frightful scenes in the horror movie. Walking next to me, Todd didn't look anxious but I suspected that he, too, was a bit shaken by what was billed as "the scariest movie ever made".

    EXAMPLE 2 **Limited Third Person:**
    The bright sunlight hurt Consuela's eyes as she emerged from the dark theater. She was still shivering from the frightful scenes in the horror movie. Walking next to her, Todd didn't look anxious but she suspected that he, too, was a bit shaken by what was billed as "the scariest movie ever made".

    EXAMPLE 3 **Omniscient Third Person:**
    The bright sunlight hurt Consuela's eyes as she emerged from the dark theater. She was still shivering from the frightful scenes in the horror movie. Walking next to her, Todd was trying not to look anxious but he, too, was a bit shaken by what was billed as "the scariest movie ever made". (Example 2 focuses on Consuela and her feelings, whereas Example 3 focuses on the feelings of both Consuela and Todd.)

Exercise 1

Determine if the following narrations are First Person (*FP*), Limited Third Person (*LTP*), or Omniscient Third Person (*OTP*).

_____ 1. Oh, the burden of trigonometry. Could anything be worse than listening to Mr. Phillips explaining the quotient rule? I shuddered to think that four more miserable months lay ahead. No medieval torture chamber could possibly have brought more agony.

_____ 2. "Wait!" she shouted, but the bus drove away without her. "How am I going to get home now?" she said to herself. She looked at a woman who was waiting for another bus. The woman smiled sadly, as if to say she was sorry.

_____ 3. I couldn't believe my eyes. There in the crowd was a friend I hadn't seen in 10 years. He saw me too! Our eyes met. But then he turned away, disappearing into the wave of humanity that was crossing Sixth Avenue.

_____ 4. Maya felt nervous as she dressed for her first date with Patrick. She didn't know he had already arrived and was waiting for her downstairs, petrified that he'd say the wrong thing to her father, who stood like a guard at the foot of the staircase.

_____ 5. Tanya looked at the new girl who had arrived at her school six weeks earlier. She'd never spoken to her. The girl was quiet and even now she was standing apart from a group of students. Tanya wondered if the girl was lonely. She would never find out. The following day the girl's family moved again. Tanya felt bad that she hadn't tried to be a friend.

_____ 6. Robert looked at his brother sitting on the bench. The coach had pulled him out of the game and he looked miserable. Robert wondered what his brother was thinking.

_____ 7. The sound was constant. *Thud! Thud! Thud!* And it was driving Alex mad. There was no escape. They were trapped, waiting for their rescuers to clear the tunnel. Natalie was frantic. Sam was badly hurt, and she wondered if they would be rescued on time.

_____ 8. Hector shook from head to toe. He had never been so afraid in his life. Why had he agreed to join the ghost hunters in that decrepit old mansion?

_____ 9. "Over here!" Monica shouted. "I think I've found something!" My heart leaped. Could it be the breakthrough we'd all been waiting for?

_____ 10. Exhausted, Carla put down her backpack. Her throat was dry and her feet burned. Above her, Mark was faring no better. His whole body ached. This was the most difficult climb they had ever made. Everyone was thinking it. Some on the team were already wondering if they should turn back.

Exercise 2

Rewrite the following narrations from the point of view of a different narrator as indicated. Then share your writing with a partner and discuss how the rewritten narration changes the feeling of the story.

1. Rewrite as a first-person narrator.

   "Goal!" shouted the referee in the last five seconds of the game, dashing the hopes of everyone on the team. Philippe couldn't believe they had lost the championship. Rene was angry. Paul felt his heart sink. They had worked so hard for this. All those hours of practice. And to lose in the last seconds was more than they could bear.

2. Rewrite as an omniscient third-person narrator.

   Day after day, the sun burned through our clothes and the work made our bodies ache. Sometimes I just wanted to take the first plane home. Martha looked like she had just lost a puppy. All these days *of digging and we hadn't found what we were looking for. Jack was the only one on the team who still sounded hopeful. He seemed so certain that we would find the hidden tomb.*

3. Rewrite as a limited third-person narrator, and give the main character a name.

    I looked over the broad expanse of desert that my sister and I had crossed as children. I felt a small pain as I thought of our parents' struggles. Next to me, my wife was also staring into the distance, perhaps thinking of her own journey to a new life so many years ago.

Exercise 3

Think of an event that happened in your childhood. Write two or three sentences describing what happened in the first person. Then rewrite the sentences in the limited third person. Rewrite them again in the omniscient third person. Read each set of sentences aloud to a partner. How does the feeling of the story change each time?

Writing an Analysis of a Short Story

Analyzing a story can help you understand it and enjoy it more. Before you write an *analysis of a short story*, you should reread the story, examine various elements of the story, and ask yourself specific questions about the following:

- **Plot.** What happens in the story? What is the sequence of events from the beginning, the middle, and the end?

- **Point of View.** Who is narrating the story? Is the narrator reliable? How does the narrator feel about what is happening in the story?

- **Character.** Who are the main characters? What makes them act in certain ways? How do other characters react to them? Do the characters have faults that cause their downfall or virtues that lead to triumph?

- **Conflict.** Is there conflict in the story (a struggle between two opposing forces)? Is the conflict internal (within the main character)? Or is the conflict external (a struggle between the main character and another character, or society, or a natural force, such as a storm)?

- **Setting.** Where and when is the story taking place? Is the setting important? If so, why? For example, a story might take place during a terrible storm that shows the weaknesses and strengths of the characters.

- **Mood.** How does the story make you feel? Is the story frightening, happy, or sad? How does mood relate to the meaning of the story?

- **Style.** Does the writer use descriptive language, figures of speech such as similes and metaphors, or irony? If so, what purpose do they serve?

- **Theme.** What is the meaning of the story? What point is the author trying to make?

Exercise 4

Analyze "The Tell-Tale Heart" by answering the following questions. Write complete sentences.

1. Write seven short sentences telling what happens in the story in the proper sequence of events.
2. Who is the narrator?
3. In Paragraphs 1 and 2, how does Poe show that we cannot trust the narrator to tell the truth?

4. As the story progresses, how do the narrator's emotions change?
5. Who are the characters in the story?
6. What fault leads to the main character's downfall?
7. Is the conflict in the story internal or external?
8. What are the opposing forces in the conflict?
9. Where does the story take place?
10. Is the setting important?
11. What is the mood of the story?
12. In Paragraphs 10 and 11, what purpose is served by Poe's use of repetition?
13. In the first three sentences of Paragraph 12, how does Poe use irony to show that the narrator isn't sane?
14. What point is Poe trying to make in this story?

Determining the Theme of a Poem

Theme is the overall meaning, or central message, that the poet wants to communicate in his or her poem. Themes are often universal topics and human struggles that affect everyone.

EXAMPLES: Youth is a time of innocence.
War causes suffering.
True love is everlasting.

- The theme of a poem is different from the subject of a poem. The **subject** is simply what the poem is about. The **theme** is the idea the poet wants to convey about the subject.

  EXAMPLES: *Subject:* Time passes quickly.
  Theme: We must make the most of the time we have.

  Subject: Life is a journey.
  Theme: We can expect both joy and suffering along the path of life.

  Subject: A sunny day
  Theme: A beautiful day brings joy to the soul.

- There are several steps you can take to help you identify a poem's theme.

  1. **Study the title.** The title gives you an idea of what the poem is about and may contain key words to help you identify the theme. For example, the title "Parting" would give you a hint that the poem might be about the pain of separation.

  2. **Determine the subject.** Read the poem through to identify what the poem is about. What scenes are described? What emotions are discussed? What images are used? For example, in the poem "To My Dear and Loving Husband" by Anne Bradstreet, she shows how much she values her husband's love by saying it is worth more than a gold mine or all the riches of the East. The subject of Bradstreet's poem is the love of husband and wife. The theme is that their love is so powerful that it will last until eternity.

  3. **Identify the speaker.** An important element to understanding a poem and determining theme is finding out who is the narrator, or speaker. Is it the first person "I" or the third person "he"? Is the speaker an individual or a group or organization? Once you identify the speaker, ask yourself: What situation is the speaker in? How does the speaker feel about the situation or subject? For example, has the speaker just lost a loved one? Is the speaker in mourning, or full of love, hate, or joy?

Exercise 5

Decide if the following sentences or phrases are Subjects (S) or Themes (T).

_____ 1. The friendship between two women

_____ 2. Change is difficult to accept

_____ 3. Love doesn't go away when a person leaves

_____ 4. Living near the beauty of the sea

_____ 5. Nighttime dreams of fame and fortune

_____ 6. It takes courage to leave home

_____ 7. Walking in the woods brings us closer to nature

_____ 8. Choices we have to make in life

_____ 9. There is always hope in times of despair

_____ 10. The painful loss of a beloved pet

Exercise 6

Analyze "If", by answering the following questions. Write complete sentences.

1. What hint does the title provide about the theme of the poem?
2. Who is the author?
3. What is the subject of the poem?
4. What images does the author use?
5. Who is the speaker?

6. What is the speaker's situation?
7. How does the speaker feel about the subject?
8. What is the meaning of the poem?
9. What is the author's purpose in writing the poem?

Writing Practice

Write an Analysis

Write an analysis of either "The Tell-Tale Heart" or "If". Review the questions and your answers to Exercise 4 for "The Tell-Tale Heart" or to Exercise 6 for "If".

Write a Rough Draft of Your Analysis

After reviewing your questions and answers, write a rough draft of your essay. Organize it in the following way:

- Begin by giving the title and the author and stating the meaning of the story or poem.
- Tell briefly what the story or poem is about.
- Discuss the story's or poem's literary elements, such as point of view, character, conflict, setting, mood, and style.
    a. Point out parts of the story or poem that convey the meaning.
    b. Quote passages and dialogs that support your statement.
- State your opinion about the story or poem. Do you think the author made his meaning clear?
- Summarize your ideas from the previous paragraphs and end your essay by restating the meaning of the story or poem.

Revise Your Rough Draft

Check the thesis statement, unity, development, coherence and purpose of your rough draft.

Edit Your Essay

Work with a partner or your teacher to edit your essay. Check the spelling, punctuation, vocabulary, and grammar.

Write Your Final Copy

After you edit your essay, you can write your final copy.

Translation

A Translate the following passage into English.

艺术在儒家眼中是道德教育的工具。道家对艺术没有正面提出系统的见解，但是他们欣赏心灵的自由流动，把自然看为崇高的理想，这给了中国艺术家极大的灵感。由于这一点，大多数中国伟大的艺术家把自然作为对象就不足为怪了。中国美术作品中的大多数杰出作品都是山水、花鸟、树木、竹枝画。在山水画里，山脚下、溪水边，往往能看见一个人，静坐沉醉在天地大美之中，从中领会超越于自然和人生之上的妙道。

B Translate the following passage into Chinese.

England is the country of Shakespeare, Milton, Byron and Dickens. The first is, by common consent, a hero of human race, a titan of literature. The other three are well-known names in most literate households. The English are inordinately proud of their language. *The Complete Oxford Dictionary* runs to 23 volumes and contains over 500,000 words. Shakespeare had a working vocabulary of over 30,000 words (some of which he made up), twice as many as a modern, educated English person. Most English people master around 8,000—the same as the vocabulary in the King James Bible. More than 80% of the Internet is written in English. English is to communication as what Microsoft is to computing: the world cannot do without it.

Weaving It Together

Unit Project

Choose one of the following topics and give a five-minute presentation based on your topic in class.

1. One or two virtues that characterize Chinese people
2. Two or three virtues that you consider important
3. An analysis of a short story you have read
4. An analysis of a poem you have read

Searching the Internet

A Search the Internet for information about the work of Rudyard Kipling. Find answers to these questions:

1. What is the title of a well-known poem by Rudyard Kipling?
2. What is the title of a short story by Rudyard Kipling?
3. What is the title of a novel written by Rudyard Kipling?
4. How many poems, short stories, and novels has he written?

B Edgar Allan Poe wrote the first detective story. Search the Internet for information about famous detective stories. Share the information with your classmates.

C You may use your research later to write an analysis of a piece of literature.

What Do You Think Now?

Refer to the very beginning of this unit. Do you know the answers now? Complete the sentence, or circle the best answer.

1. A first-person narrator (knows/does not know) what all the characters are doing in a story.
2. All stories (are/are not) written from the same point of view.
3. The title of a poem helps us to understand its _____.
4. The theme of a poem is not the same as the _____.

Broadening Your Horizon

A

Who Was Edgar Ellan Poe?

The name Poe brings to mind images of murderers and madmen, premature burials, and mysterious women who return from the dead.

B

Rudyard Kipling

Rudyard Kipling is one of the best-known of the late Victorian poets and storytellers. Although he was awarded the Nobel Prize for literature in 1907, his unpopular political views caused his work to be neglected shortly after his death.

C

The Raven

"Once upon a midnight dreary, while I pondered, weak and weary,

Over many a quaint and curious volume of forgotten lore—"

Unit 8 Readings from Literature

GLOSSARY

A

acceptance	n.	赞同，赞成	U1R1
(as) much as		尽管（指尽管某一情况是事实，而另一情况也是事实）	U1R1
(up) for sale		待售	U1R2
accustom	v.	使适应；使习惯	U2R2
additive	n.	添加剂；添加物	U6R1
adoption	n.	采用，采纳	U1R1
adulterate	v.	食物掺假	U6R1
adversarial	a.	对手的，敌对的	U5R1
advocate	n.	提倡者，拥护者，鼓吹者	U6R2
affectionate	a.	亲切的，有感情的	U1R2
agent	n.	（化学）剂；作用剂	U6R1
agony	n.	极大的痛苦/苦恼	U8R1
alarming	a.	使人害怕的，扰乱人心的；使人惊慌的	U6R1
all along		自始至终	U5R1
allowance	n.	(make ~) 体谅	U8R2
alter	v.	使变化，改变	U1R1
amnesty	n.	特赦	U3R2
anoint	v.	（尤指宗教仪式中）涂擦油于（头上或身上）	U2R1
anointment	n.	涂擦油	U2R1
antelope	n.	羚羊	U3R1
appetizing	a.	促进食欲的；开胃的	U6R1
apply	v.	(~ to) 适用于（某人、某种情况）；有效	U5R2
archaeological	a.	考古学的	U2R1
archaeology	n.	考古学	U2R1
around the clock		日以继夜地；连续一整天	U3R2
assassinate	n.	暗杀，行刺	U7R1
at one's worst		最差的一面；在情况最糟糕的时候	U3R1
atrocity	n.	暴行；残暴	U3R2
attendant	n.	服务员；侍者；随从	U2R1
aversive	a.	令人嫌恶的；令人厌恶的	U4R2
awareness	n.	意识，认识	U3R2

B

bachelor	n.	学士	U5R2
bandwagon	n.	(jump on the ~) 赶浪头，顺应潮流，随大流	U1R1

barefoot	a.	赤脚的	U3R1
base... on		以……为基础，以……为根据	U5R2
be loaded with		充斥着（某素质、态度等）；充满……（尤指不好的东西）	U6R1
be off base		大错特错；与事实不符	U4R2
beverage	n.	饮料	U6R1
biotech	n.	生物技术	U6R2
boast	v.	自夸，夸耀	U2R1
boredom	n.	厌烦；厌倦	U4R2
bottomless	a.	无底的；深不可测的	U3R1
bring about		引起；导致；造成；带来	U5R1
bubble	n.	气泡；水泡	U2R2
bud	n.	(taste ~s) 味蕾	U6R1
bullet	n.	子弹	U3R1
buy up		（迅速地）囤积，大量买下（土地、票券、食品等）	U6R1

C

caffeine	n.	咖啡碱；咖啡因	U4R2
campaign	v.	参与一系列活动以到达某种政治或商业的目的	U7R2
captivity	n.	(in ~) 被俘，拘禁，囚禁；束缚	U7R2
cart	v.	(~ off) 带走，抓走（尤指进监狱）	U1R2
catch on		流行	U1R1
chaotic	a.	混乱的，毫无秩序的	U1R1
chill	v.	使（某人）感到冷；使（某人）不寒而栗	U8R1
chimpanzee	n.	（同chimp）黑猩猩	U7R2
choleric	a.	易怒的；暴躁的；（黄）胆汁质的	U4R1
clause	n.	（法律等文件中的）条款，项目	U7R2
closely	ad.	密切地，紧密地	U3R2
co-founder	n.	共同创立者	U3R2
colonel	n.	（陆军、海军陆战队或美国空军的）上校军衔；上校	U1R1
coloring	n.	着色剂	U6R1
combination	n.	结合，联合；混合	U1R1
commoner	n.	平民	U2R1
compassion	n.	怜悯；同情	U3R1
competitive	a.	竞争（竞赛）的；取决于竞争（竞赛）的	U5R1
complain	v.	抱怨；不满，发牢骚	U1R1
complexity	n.	复杂性，错综复杂	U1R1
complicated	a.	复杂的；费解的；棘手的	U5R1

GLOSSARY

compose	v.	(be ~d of) 由……组成	U4R1
conceive	v.	构想出; 想出; 设想	U5R2
conglomeration	n.	混合物	U6R1
conquer	v.	征服	U1R1
conscious	a.	关注的; 注重的; 有意识的	U4R1
consequently	ad.	因而, 所以	U4R2
consistency	n.	连贯性, 前后一致	U1R1
contact	n.	联系; 联络	U4R2
contaminate	v.	污染; 毒害	U6R1
contemplative	a.	沉思的; 冥想的; 默想的	U2R2
contribute	v.	(~ to) 促成, 有助于	U6R2
cooperative	a.	协作的, 合作的	U5R1
coordinate	v.	调整; 整合	U3R2
core	n.	（事物的）核心, 最重要部分	U2R2
cosmetics	n.	化妆品	U7R2
count on		期望, 指望	U6R1
cover up		遮盖, 覆盖	U2R1
crisis	n.	危机	U3R2
crisp	n.	油炸（马铃）薯片	U1R2
crispy	a.	脆的; 酥脆的; 鲜脆的	U6R1
critical	a.	(~ of) 吹毛求疵的; 批评严厉的	U5R1
crucial	a.	至关重要的, 关键性的	U3R2
currently	ad.	现时, 当前	U6R1
customary	a.	（人）习惯性的	U1R2

D

date back to		自……存在至今, 追溯到……年代	U2R1
deal in		卷入; 感兴趣	U8R2
decentralize	v.	分散（行政权）	U3R2
definition	n.	定义; 限定; 确定（尤指词或短语）	U2R1
deodorant	n.	除（尤指人体的）臭剂	U2R1
derogatory	a.	侮辱的, 贬义的	U7R1
descend	v.	下来; 下降	U2R2
dialect	n.	方言, 地方话, 土话	U1R1
discriminate	v.	歧视	U7R2
displace	v.	转移	U3R1
display	n.	（物品的）展示, 陈列	U1R2

distribution	n.	分布；分配	U4R1
documentary	n.	纪录片	U3R1
dominant	a.	强大的；有优势的；突出的	U4R1
dramatic	a.	给人深刻印象的；突然的；惊人的	U1R1
dubious	a.	似乎不诚信的，不安全的；不确定的，可疑的；半信半疑的	U7R1
dye	n.	染料，染色	U6R1

E

effective	a.	产生预期效果的；有效的	U3R2
effectiveness	n.	效果	U3R2
efficiency	n.	效率；效能	U1R1
elementary	a.	初步的，基本的	U5R2
embark	v.	(~ upon) 开始，着手（尤指新的、有难度且费时的事）	U1R2
enclosed	a.	被（围墙、篱笆等）围住的，封闭的	U7R1
end up		结果为……；以……结束（尤指意料之外）	U1R1
endow	v.	(be ~ed with) 天生赋有	U7R2
endurance	n.	忍耐；耐性	U3R1
enforce	v.	执行，实施（法律）	U7R1
engineering	n.	工程（学）	U6R2
enhance	v.	提高，增加；加强	U6R1
enterprising	a.	有事业心的；有进取心的；有开创精神的	U4R1
entitle	v.	(be ~d to) 有权利、有资格（去享有，去做）	U7R2
essentially	ad.	实质上；本质上；根本上	U4R2
establish	v.	建立，设立	U1R1
evolve	v.	（使）逐步发展；（使）逐渐演变	U1R1
excess	a.	过量的，额外的	U6R2
executive	n.	（公司或商业机构中的）主管，行政人员	U7R2
exhausting	a.	使人精疲力竭的	U2R1
exhibit	v.	展出，展览	U1R2
expertise	n.	专长；专业知识	U2R1
extend	v.	（指空间、土地或时间）延伸；继续	U2R1
extensive	a.	大规模的；大量的	U2R1
extent	n.	(to such an ~ that) 达到如此程度	U2R1
extravagant	a.	（花钱）浪费的，无必要的	U2R2
extraversion	n.	外向性；外倾性	U4R2
extravert	n.	性格外向的人；好交际的人	U4R2

GLOSSARY

F

facilitate	v.	促进；使便利	U7R1
factor	n.	因素（任何相互作用而产生某种结果的力量, 状况, 影响等）	U5R1
fake	a.	假的, 冒充的	U6R1
fanaticism	n.	（如同政治或宗教领域的）狂热, 盲信	U1R1
fashion	n.	（衣服、头发等的）流行式样；（行为等的）时髦；时尚	U1R1
faucet	n.	水龙头；旋塞	U2R2
feature	v.	（在电影、杂志、表演等中）介绍, 特载；特别推出；以……为主要内容	U7R1
femininity	n.	女性；女子气	U5R2
figure	v.	（以重要地位）出现	U1R1
file	v.	把（投诉信、法律案件、正式文件等）登记在案；正式提出	U6R1
film	n.	薄层, 薄膜	U8R1
filth	n.	肮脏；污物	U2R1
flavoring	n.	调味品, 调味料	U6R1
fluid	n.	流体；液体；流质	U4R1
for one thing		其中一个原因是	U1R1
force	n.	（为某个目的而训练和组织的）一群人, 队伍, 群体	U3R2
fund	n.	基金；专款；资金	U7R1
furthermore	ad.	而且；再者；另外还有	U5R1

G

game	n.	猎物	U7R1
gaol	n.	监狱	U1R2
gender	n.	性别	U5R2
generalization	n.	一般化；普通化；概论	U5R1
genetic	a.	遗传的；基因的	U6R2
get carried away		忘乎所以, 忘形	U1R1
give off		发出；放出；散发出；放射出	U6R1
give way to		屈服	U8R2
go after		追逐	U3R1
gorilla	n	大猩猩	U7R2
grace	n.	优美；优雅	U4R1
grate	v.	磨碎, 压碎	U6R1
gratitude	n.	感激之情；谢意	U5R1
grave	a.	严重的；令人担忧的	U2R1
gum	n.	树胶	U6R1

H

hang over		（不愉快的事）逼近；威胁着	U3R1
harsh	a.	刺耳的	U5R1
hastily	ad.	飞快地；仓促地	U2R2
haul	n.	(long ~) 漫长而艰苦的旅程（工作，活动等）	U6R1
herd	n.	（同一种类或一同栖息的）兽群	U3R1
hide	n.	（用于制成皮革的）兽皮	U1R2
hierarchically	a.	分层；分等级地	U4R2
hip	n.	臀部；髋部	U4R1
hold on		坚持下去	U8R2
hot-tempered	a.	暴躁的；性急的；易怒的	U4R1
humane	a.	人道的	U7R2
humanitarian	a.	人道主义的	U3R2
husk	n.	荚，壳	U6R1
hygiene	n.	卫生	U2R1
hyper-	prefix	过分（的），过度（的）	U6R2

I

ideal	n.	(~ of) 完美典型，典范	U5R2
imagery	n.	意象，画像	U3R2
implant	v.	移植；植入	U6R2
implication	n.	(have ~s for) 给（计划、行为或事件）带来（需要考虑或讨论的）可能的影响，可能的后果；含义；暗示	U7R2
impulsive	a.	易冲动的；莽撞的	U4R2
in one way		在某种程度上	U5R1
in reference to		关于（尤用于公函）	U1R2
incredible	a.	惊人的，奇妙的；好得难以置信的	U7R1
indefensible	a.	不可原谅的；无法辩解的	U7R1
indifferent	a.	（尤指对别人的困难或感情）不关心，不在乎	U1R1
individual	a.	个人的，个体的	U5R2
indoor	a.	在室内使用的，户内的	U2R1
indulge	v.	(~ in) （让自己）享受一下；（使自己）沉溺于	U2R1
infant	n.	婴儿	U5R1
infest	v.	（有害的、危险的、讨厌的东西）大批出没于；侵扰；骚扰	U2R1
ingest	v.	咽下	U6R1
inherent	a.	内在的，密不可分的	U7R2

Glossary 213

GLOSSARY

injection	n.	注射；注射剂	U6R2
instance	n.	例子	U1R1
insult	n.	辱骂，凌辱；侮辱性的言行	U7R1
integral	a.	（用于构成整体）必需的，不可缺少的	U2R2
integrate	v.	（使）合并	U3R2
interaction	n.	相互作用；相互影响；相互配合	U5R1
internal	a.	内部的，里面的	U6R1
intimate	a.	亲密的；亲近的	U4R2
introspective	a.	内省的；反省的	U4R2
introversion	n.	内向性；内倾性	U4R2
invade	v.	侵扰（某人）	U1R1
invaluable	a.	极有价值的	U7R1
investigation	n.	调查，研究	U6R1
involved	a.	(be ~ in) 参与某活动/某事件；与某活动/某事件有关	U7R1
irrelevant	a.	不相关的，无关紧要的	U7R1
issue	v.	正式发行（新邮票、硬币、股票等）	U1R1
issue	n.	问题；议题	U7R2
item	n.	条款；项目	U2R1

J

jumbo	n./a.	庞然大物/（同类中）特大的，巨大的	U1R2
just about		几乎	U6R1

K

keep an eye out for		当心，警惕	U3R1
keep up		（进展，学习等）跟上（某人），不落后	U1R1

L

launch	v.	发动，发起，开始进行	U7R1
lawmaker	n.	立法者，立法官员	U7R2
lawsuit	n.	诉讼；诉讼案件	U6R1
leadership	n.	领导才能；领导素质	U3R1
lean	a.	苗条而健美的	U4R1
legendary	a.	非常有名的，大名鼎鼎的；传奇式的	U1R2
lengthy	a.	长时间的；过长的	U2R1
let alone		更不用说，更谈不上	U1R2

liberal	a.	（对别人的想法、意见、感情）宽宏大度的，开明的	U1R1
lifesaving	a.	救命的；救生用的	U3R2
light up		照亮，使生辉	U3R2
limb	n.	肢；臂；腿	U4R1
livestock	n.	家畜，牲畜	U6R2
logistics	n.	物流	U3R2
long	v.	渴望；热望	U3R1
loofah	n.	（洗澡用的）丝瓜络	U2R2
lose one's temper		发脾气	U4R1
lump	n.	块，团	U6R1
luxury	n.	豪华；华贵；奢侈	U2R1

M

magnet	n.	磁铁；磁石，吸铁石	U1R1
magnificent	a.	宏伟的；壮观的	U2R1
maintain	v.	坚持认为；主张	U4R2
major	v.	（在大学）主修	U5R2
make one's point		说服别人赞成自己的观点	U5R1
make up		编造	U1R1
makeup	n.	化妆品	U5R2
manufacturer	n.	制造商，制造厂	U6R1
marine	n	水兵；（英国皇家海军或美国海军的）海军陆战队员	U3R2
masculinity	n.	男性；男子气	U5R2
mean	a.	卑鄙的；不善良的；刻薄的	U4R1
medicinal	a.	（医）药的；药用的；有疗效的	U2R1
melancholic	a.	忧郁的；抑郁的；黑胆汁质的	U4R1
merge	v.	合并；融合	U1R1
metabolize	v.	使发生新陈代谢	U6R1
meticulous	a.	非常注意细节的；作风谨慎的	U4R1
military	a.	军事的；军人的	U3R1
misquote	v.	错误地引证，误引（他人的话）	U1R2
mobilize	v.	争取支持/动用资源等；动员起来	U3R2
mold	n.	霉	U6R1
momentum	n.	动力，势头	U1R1
mood	n.	心情；心境；情绪	U2R2
more (to something) than meets the eye		（某些事情）不是一眼就能看得出来的	U5R1

GLOSSARY

moreover	ad.	此外,而且,加之,再者	U1R1
multimedia	a.	多媒体的	U3R2
muscle	n.	肌肉	U2R2

N

necessity	n.	必需品	U2R2
negative	a.	消极的	U5R2
nerve	n.	神经	U2R2
neuroticism	n.	神经质；具有不稳定、焦虑及有侵略性等的特征	U4R2
nevertheless	ad.	然而,不过；尽管如此	U5R1
nickname	n.	（尤指给朋友或家人取的）绰号,外号；诨名	U1R2
nicotine	n.	烟碱；尼古丁	U4R2
nonprofit	a.	非盈利的	U3R1
numerous	a.	许多的,很多的	U1R1

O

oblige	v.	使（某人）非做……不可,迫使；责成	U7R2
occasion	n.	时节；时刻	U2R1
occupy	v.	占据,占有	U3R2
odor	n.	气味（尤指臭味）	U2R1
olive	n.	（生长在地中海国家的）橄榄树；橄榄	U2R1
ongoing	a.	继续进行的；不断发展中的	U1R1
online	a.	（计算机）联机的,（与计算机）联线的	U5R1
onset	n.	（尤指某种不好事情的）开始,发作	U1R1
opponent	n.	反对者	U7R1
option	n.	选项,选择	U3R2
or rather		更确切地说	U2R1
organic	n./a.	有机食物/不使用化肥的,有机的	U6R2
original	a.	原先的,最早的,最初的	U1R2
outfitter	n.	旅行用品商店,户外活动（如露营）用品店	U7R1
outlaw	v.	将……定为非法,全面禁止	U7R1
outraged	a.	愤怒的,震惊的	U7R1
outright	ad.	完全地,彻底地	U5R2
outwit	v.	以智取胜	U3R2
overhaul	n.	（对机器的）大检修；（对体制的）彻底改革	U7R1
overtake	v.	（发展或增长）赶超	U7R1
overtones	n.	（情感或态度）含蓄的表示；暗示；弦外之音	U2R1

overwhelm	v.	（工作，问题等）使应接不暇，压垮	U4R2
owe sth. to sb.		把……归功于，有……是由于	U1R2

P

palate	n.	味觉	U6R1
pale	a.	浅的，淡的	U8R1
pass down		传给（后代）；传下来	U2R2
penetrate	v.	进入；渗入；刺入；穿过，穿透	U2R2
persevering	a.	不屈不挠的，坚韧的	U3R1
personality	n.	（因常出现在报纸、电视等上而知名的）名人	U7R1
petition	n.	请愿（书）	U7R1
philanthropist	n.	慈善家，乐善好施者	U1R1
phlegm	n.	粘液；痰	U4R1
phlegmatic	a.	冷静的；沉着的；镇定的	U4R1
phonetic	a.	使用音标代表语音的，表示发音的	U1R1
phonographic	a.	表音速记的	U1R1
physiological	a.	生理学的	U4R2
pinch	n.	一撮盐/胡椒粉等	U1R1
pitch-and-toss	n.	掷硬币游戏	U8R2
plumbing	n.	（尤指建筑物中的）管件总称	U2R1
plump	a.	丰满的；胖乎乎的；圆滚滚的	U6R1
plunge	v.	投入；跳入；冲进	U2R1
poacher	n.	偷猎者，偷捕者	U7R1
pop	v.	(~ up) 突然（意外）地出现，冒出来	U1R1
popularity	n.	流行，普及，受欢迎；声望	U1R2
positive	a.	（指人）（对某事）确信的；肯定的	U2R1
prehistoric	a.	史前的，有历史记载以前的	U4R1
prescribed	a.	规定的	U2R2
preservative	n.	防腐剂	U6R1
preserve	n.	私人渔猎区	U7R1
prevail	v.	胜（过），（对……）占上风	U7R2
primarily	ad.	主要地	U1R1
prime	n.	(in one's ~) 正值盛年，在壮年时期，风华正茂	U7R1
productive	a.	多产的，丰饶的	U6R2
propose	v.	提出（某观点，方法等）	U4R1
protein	n.	蛋白（质）	U6R1
prototypic	a.	典型的；原型的	U4R2

GLOSSARY

puberty	n.	青春期	U6R2
purge	v.	清除（有害或不可接受的东西）	U7R1
purification	n.	净化；提纯	U2R1
pursuit	n.	(~ of) 追求	U7R2
put-down	n.	贬低（轻蔑）的话	U5R1

R

rampant	a.	（指犯罪、疾病、信仰等）蔓延的；不可控制的	U2R1
rational	a.	（原因）合理的，基于理性的	U1R1
ravage	v.	毁坏；摧毁；使荒废	U3R2
raven	n.	渡鸦	U2R2
real time		实时	U3R2
reassure	v.	使安心，使消除疑虑	U6R2
refine	v.	改进，改善	U3R2
refrain	v.	(~ from) 节制，克制；避免；制止	U7R1
refreshing	a.	消除疲劳的，提神的；清凉的	U2R1
refugee	n.	难民，避难者	U3R1
regime	n.	政权，政体	U3R2
regulate	v.	控制，管理	U6R2
relating to		有关，涉及	U2R1
release	v.	释放，放出	U7R1
remarkably	ad.	不寻常地；突出地	U5R2
repress	v.	抑制；控制	U2R1
resettle	v.	（使）在新的地方定居	U3R1
residue	n.	残余，残渣；余渣，残余物	U6R1
resilient	a.	能复原的；有复原力的	U3R1
resolution	n.	分辨率	U3R2
resounding	a.	（声音）响亮的，洪亮的	U5R1
resource	n.	资源	U3R2
responder	n.	应急反应者	U3R2
retardation	n.	延迟；减缓；落后；迟缓	U6R1
retiring	a.	孤僻的；不合群的	U4R2
retreat	n.	安静的地方；隐退的处所	U2R1
rinse	v.	冲洗	U2R1
ritual	n.	仪式（程序）；例行习惯	U2R1
roam	v.	闲逛，漫步；漫游	U7R1
rub	v.	磨；擦；搓；揉	U2R1

S

salmon	n.	鲑，三文鱼	U6R2
sandpaper	n.	砂纸	U3R1
sanguine	a.	充满信心的；乐观的	U4R1
sanitation	n.	（环境）卫生；卫生设备	U2R1
sarcasm	n.	讽刺，挖苦，嘲笑	U5R1
savvy	n.	实际知识；见识	U3R2
scheme	n.	（用以组织信息、思想等的）系统，体系	U4R2
scoop	v.	（用勺子或手）舀出；捧起，掬起	U2R2
scrape	v.	刮；擦；削	U2R1
scrub	v.	用力擦净	U2R1
seek out		找出，找到	U4R2
seizure	n.	（心脏病等疾病的）突然发作	U6R1
self-assured	a.	自信的	U5R1
self-conscious	n.	（因顾虑他人看法而）忸怩（作态）的，害羞的，不自然的	U5R1
sensation	n.	轰动，激动；引起轰动的人（事）	U1R2
sensation	n.	（感官的）感觉；（尤指）触觉	U2R2
sensitivity	n.	敏感；敏感性	U4R2
shadow	n.	残余；痕迹	U1R1
shampoo	v.	用洗发剂洗	U2R2
shed	v.	去掉（不需要或不想要的东西）；（动物或植物）使（外皮、毛发、叶子等）蜕下，脱落，剥落	U1R1
shriek	v.	尖叫；叫喊	U3R1
slip	v.	（指物体）意外滑离原位	U8R1
slip by		溜走，悄悄地走	U2R1
soak	v.	（使）浸；泡	U2R2
soapsuds	n.	肥皂泡沫	U2R2
sociable	a.	喜欢与人交往的；好交际的	U4R1
sociologist	n.	社会学家	U5R2
solitude	n.	（尤指令人惬意的）独居，独处	U4R2
solution	n.	溶液	U6R1
solve	v.	解释，解答，解决	U5R1
somehow	ad.	由于某种不明原因，不知为什么；用某种方法；不知怎么地	U3R1
sophisticated	a.	复杂的；不易懂的	U2R1
spatial	a.	（关于）空间的	U5R1
spice	n.	（为某事增添）趣味，情趣，风味	U1R1
spine	n.	脊柱；脊椎	U4R1

GLOSSARY

splash	v.	（使）溅落；（使）飞溅	U2R1
splendor	n.	华丽；壮丽	U2R1
spoil	v.	变质	U6R1
sponge	n.	（擦洗用的）海绵（块）	U2R2
squeaky	a.	发出短促而尖利声音的；吱吱叫的	U2R1
squeaky clean		极其干净的	U2R1
stack	v.	整齐地堆起；（使）成堆；摞起	U6R1
stackable	a.	容易整齐堆起的	U6R1
stalk	v.	（为捉拿或杀死某人或某动物而）悄悄地跟踪；潜近	U7R1
stamp	n.	印章，图章；印记，戳记	U6R2
standby	n.	备用品	U3R2
start out		启程；开始（着手）做	U3R1
stereotype	v.	对……产生成见；把……模式化	U4R1
stiff	a.	（身体）僵硬的，酸痛的	U4R1
stir	v.	(~ up) 惹起（麻烦），挑起（争吵）	U7R1
stool	n.	凳子	U2R2
stoop	v.	俯身；弯腰	U4R1
strategy	n.	策略；计谋；行动计划	U4R2
stride	n.	大步；阔步	U4R1
stringent	a.	（法律、规则、条件）严格的，严厉的，受严格约束的	U6R2
stroke	n.	（钢笔或毛笔的）一挥，挥笔动作	U1R1
stuff	v.	填满，装满	U1R2
subconsciously	ad.	（思维，感情等）下意识地，潜意识地，有模糊意识地	U5R2
subject	n.	（君主国的）臣民，国民	U1R2
subsidize	v.	给……津贴（补贴）	U7R1
substance	n.	物质	U6R1
subsume	v.	把……归入；把……包括在内	U4R2
subtle	a.	微妙的；不易察觉的	U4R2
sustainable	a.	可持续的，不破坏环境的	U7R1
sweepings	n.	扫拢的垃圾（尘土等）	U6R1
sweetener	n.	甜味剂	U6R1
synthetic	a.	合成的；人造的	U6R1

T

take on		接受（工作等）；承担（责任等）	U5R2
take... seriously		重视，认真对待	U5R2
take... into account		把……考虑在内	U7R2

tap	v.	（用手或脚）轻敲，轻叩，轻拍		U4R1
tech-savvy	a.	精通技术的		U3R2
temperament	n.	性格；性情		U4R1
tend to		照料；护理；服侍		U5R2
thermal	a.	热的；产生热的；热引起的		U2R1
thorn	n.	刺，棘刺，荆棘		U6R1
threaten	v.	威胁；恐吓		U3R1
timid	a.	胆小的；胆怯的；羞怯的		U4R1
tingling	a.	感到刺痛的		U2R2
tint	v.	染色，着色于……；染（发）		U6R1
torso	n.	（头和四肢除外的）人体躯干		U4R1
touch on		与……有关；（说话或写作时）简略地提到，提及		U7R1
toxic	a.	有毒的		U6R1
transfer	v.	搬运；迁移		U1R2
treat sb. to sth.		使某人享受某物		U2R1
treaty	n.	（国家或政府间的）条约		U7R2
trial	n.	磨练		U3R1
triumph	n.	（尤其指苦战后获得的）胜利，成功，成就		U8R2
trophy	n.	（尤指战争或狩猎中的）战利品，猎获物，胜利纪念品		U7R1
trustworthy	a.	值得信赖的，可靠的		U4R1
tsunami	n.	海啸		U3R2
tumor	n.	瘤		U6R1
turn out		结果（是），原来（是），证明（是）		U5R1
tweet	n.	运用推特社交网络发送的信息		U3R2
twofold	a.	有两部分的；双重的		U2R2

U

unalienable	a.	（同 inalienable）（权利）不可剥夺的	U7R2
unconscious	a.	（感情）无意识的，未意识到的	U4R1
uniform	a.	全部相同的，一致的	U1R1
uninhibited	a.	无拘束的；不受禁止的	U4R2
unscrupulous	a.	不择手段的；不讲道德的；无耻的	U1R2
unwind	v.	放松；松弛	U2R2

V

varied	a.	各种各样的；不同的	U2R1

GLOSSARY

vengeful	a.	怀有深仇大恨的, 图谋报复的, 复仇的	U5R1
vermin	n.	害虫, 寄生虫（如跳蚤, 虱子等）	U2R1
viable	a.	可望成功的, 切合实际的	U5R2
vigorously	ad.	强有力地; 积极地	U2R2
vine	n.	藤本植物, 攀缘植物	U6R1
virtually	ad.	几乎; 差不多	U2R1
virtuous	a.	品德高尚的; 有道德的; 善良的	U2R1
vitamin	n.	维生素; 维他命	U6R1
vowel	n.	元音字母（英语的元音字母为a, e, i, o, u, 有时也包括y）; 元音	U1R1
vulture	n.	秃鹫	U8R1

W

waterproof	a.	防水的; 不透水的	U2R2
weigh down		重压（某人）; 压弯了（某人）的腰	U4R1
wilderness	n.	荒地	U3R1
will	n.	遗嘱	U1R1
wind up		（意外地）(以……)告终; 落得个(……的下场)	U6R2
wire	v.	基因决定	U6R2
within the reach of		伸手可及	U2R1
wrongdoing	n.	不道德的行为, 不法勾当; 坏事	U5R1

Y

year-round	a.	全年的	U6R2
yield	v.	生产; 产生	U4R2
youngster	n.	年轻人	U1R2

Z

zoologist	n.	动物学家	U7R2